Employment Law

Melanie Slocombe

Employment Law
by Melanie Slocombe

1st edition 1997
2nd edition 1998
3rd edition 1999
4th edition 2000
    Reprinted 2001
5th edition 2002
    Reprinted 2002
6th edition 2003
    Reprinted 2003
    Reprinted 2004
7th edition 2004
8th edition 2005

© 2005 Lawpack Publishing

Lawpack Publishing Limited
76–89 Alscot Road
London SE1 3AW

www.lawpack.co.uk

ISBN: 1 904053 92 0

The contents of this book have been approved under Scottish law by Neill Clerk & Murray, Solicitors.

Exclusion of Liability and Disclaimer

For convenience (and for no other reason) 'him', 'he' and 'his' have been used throughout and should be read to include 'her', 'she' and 'her'.

Contents

Important facts

This book contains the information, advice and example contracts and letters to help maintain employer/employee relations in line with the law and codes of practice.

The information this book contains has been carefully compiled from professional sources, but its accuracy is not guaranteed, as laws and regulations may change or be subject to differing interpretations.

Neither this nor any other publication can take the place of a solicitor on important legal matters. As with any legal matter, common sense should determine whether you need the assistance of a solicitor, rather than rely solely on the information in this book.

This book can be read in relation to England & Wales and Scotland; any differences in law are highlighted. The law is stated as at 1 April 2005.

About the author

Melanie Slocombe is a partner at solicitors McDermott, Will & Emery, a leading international law firm. She qualified as a solicitor in 1995 and joined MW&E in 1999.

Melanie is an experienced employment tribunal advocate, and has also brought and defended proceedings in the High Court and in the Court of Appeal. Melanie regularly advises on corporate transactions and on pan-European human resource issues. Her clients include large plc organisations as well as a number of senior executives. She regularly gives in-house and client training seminars, and writes for PLC and other legal publishers. In addition to this book, Melanie has also written *Employment Law Made Easy* and the *Employment Contracts Kit*, both published by Lawpack.

How to use this book

This book can help you achieve an important legal objective conveniently, efficiently and economically. Remember that it is important for you to use this book properly if you are to avoid later difficulties.

Step-by-step instructions for using this book

1. Read this book carefully. If, after thorough examination, you decide that your requirements are not met by this book, or you do not feel confident about writing your own documents, consult a solicitor.

2. Each chapter of this book provides an overview of the background, current legislation and codes of practice relating to different areas of employment law which employers and employees ought to know about.

3. An employer is obliged to draw up and maintain certain employee records and to know about employment procedures. At the end of this book are Appendices containing example letters, an employment contract and notices. These are template documents, with important footnotes, for reference when drawing up your own. Employment-related procedure flowcharts are also included.

4. Always use a pen or type on legal documents; never use pencil.

5. Employer and employee should keep signed copies.

6. Do not cross out or erase anything on your final documents.

7. You will find a helpful glossary of terms at the end of this book. Refer to this glossary if you find unfamiliar terms.

8. Always keep legal documents in a safe place and in a location known to your company secretary and solicitor.

Introduction

Few legal fields change as rapidly as employment law. New statutes influenced by case law, economic policy changes, trade union practices, government intervention and the tremendous impact of membership of the European Union and the European Court of Justice all mean that employment law is constantly being tested, reshaped and redefined. This in turn affects the relationship between employer and employee and both parties need to be aware of their rights and duties. All employees have a right to know what law protects them in the workplace; and employers should know how changes in the law could affect their companies. The idea of seeking legal remedies through confrontation in the courts for violations of employment law has become increasingly acceptable in recent years.

The plethora of new legislation in the UK is intended to replace the notion of conflict between employers and employees with the promotion of partnership and the encouragement of flexible working. While the notion of partnership and flexible working should be encouraged, the practical effect of the new legislation is to increase individual rights and place an even greater responsibility on the employer to ensure that it complies with its new 'employee-friendly' obligations.

In addition, since 2 October 2000, the Human Rights Act 1998 has been in force, incorporating the European Convention on Human Rights and Freedoms (1993) into English, Welsh and Scots law (although the Scotland Act 1988 had already brought into force the provisions of the European Convention to some extent) and this is permeating into most areas of the law, including employment law. The rights that have most relevance to employment law are: the right to a fair trial, private and family life, freedom of thought, conscience and religion, freedom of expression, freedom of assembly and prohibition of discrimination. The Act is not directly enforceable in proceedings brought against a body in the private sector, but the Act has an indirect effect on the outcome because courts and tribunals are obliged to interpret UK legislation so as to conform to the Convention.

Because the growth of email, voicemail and other office-based communications has changed the way in which people work, the need to monitor employees in the use of such communications has become necessary for employers to run their business. This needs to be balanced against the right of employees to privacy.

The Human Rights Act 1998 gives rise to some interesting issues surrounding the monitoring of telephone calls and email. In the meantime, the government has moved to address concerns about the legality of surveillance/monitoring of employees by implementing the Telecommunications (Lawful Business Practice) (Interception of Communications) Regulations 2000.

One of the purposes of this book is to promote good communications in the workplace. It may draw your attention to areas of potential or actual conflict. When they arise, disputes can usually be resolved through deliberate, honest negotiation. No employer enjoys having to take disciplinary action – let alone dismiss an employee – because of the sense of failure it frequently brings on both sides. But if dismissal is the only course of action, it must be done in a legally acceptable way.

This book provides a broad overview of employment regulations, rights and duties for both employers and employees. It will alert you to the conditions, practices, responsibilities, duties and remedies that fall within the scope of employment law, and help you navigate your way through them.

Melanie Slocombe

CHAPTER 1

Recruitment

Recruitment is divided into two main sections in this chapter: the first on the legal requirements behind recruitment and the second, beginning on page 9, on recruitment guidelines and codes of good practice.

Legal requirements

When recruiting staff, it is very important that an employer complies with the legal requirements – in particular relating to discrimination – as laid down in legislation. The legal requirements that are dealt with in this chapter are:

- Discrimination
- Employees' past criminal convictions
- Employing children and young persons
- Restrictions on employing women
- Employment of EU and EEA nationals
- Employment of non-EU nationals

Discrimination

This chapter deals with discrimination during the recruitment process.

Chapter 5 takes a broader view of discrimination in employment, its definition and the legal recourse available to employees who feel they have been unlawfully discriminated against.

No matter whether employers are recruiting through employment agencies, job centres, careers offices or schools, they have a duty not to discriminate. They must not give instructions or bring pressure to discriminate.

Discrimination on the grounds of sex, race or marital status

It is unlawful for employers to advertise vacancies, select interview candidates or offer employment in a way that discriminates on the grounds of sex (including gender reassignment), race or marital status.

An employee or job applicant who feels that he has been discriminated against on any of these grounds can raise a complaint with the Equal Opportunities Commission, the Commission for Racial Equality or an employment tribunal.

Exceptions

There are some jobs for which the sex or race of the successful candidate may be a 'genuine occupational qualification' and in these circumstances discrimination in advertisements, in the interview procedure, in job offers, in offers of promotion or in training or transfers is acceptable.

1. **Sex:** A person's sex is a 'genuine occupational qualification' for a job in the following circumstances:

    - where the essential nature of the job calls for someone of a certain sex for reason of **physiology** (e.g. a female model);

    - where it is necessary to preserve **decency or privacy** because the job is likely to involve physical contact with people of the opposite sex in circumstances where those people may reasonably object to the job holder being of the opposite sex, or because the holder of the job is likely to do work in the presence of people who are in a state of undress or are using sanitary facilities and therefore might reasonably object to the presence of a person of the opposite sex;

- where the nature or location of the job means that the job holder must **live in** the premises provided by the employer. Because it is impractical for him to live anywhere else and the premises are not equipped with separate sleeping accommodation or sanitary facilities for men and women, it is unreasonable to expect the employer to equip the premises with such accommodation or facilities;

- where the job is in a **single-sex establishment** or single-sex part of an establishment for people requiring special care, supervision or attention, and the essential character of that establishment or that part makes it reasonable to restrict the job to a person of the same sex as those for whom the establishment (or that part of it) exists;

- where the job is for the provision of **personal services** to people in order to promote their welfare, education or other similar services and those services can more effectively be provided by someone of a certain sex;

- where the job involves **working outside the UK** in a country whose laws and customs are such that the duties could not, or could not effectively, be performed by a man (or by a woman);

- where the job is one of two held by a **married couple**.

2. **Race:** A person's race is a 'genuine occupational qualification' for a job in the following circumstances:

- where the job involves **dramatic performance** and someone of a particular racial group is required for authenticity;

- where the job involves working as a **model** for producing works of art, a picture or film and a person of a racial group is needed for authenticity;

- where the job involves working in a **restaurant** open to the public in a particular setting for which someone of a particular racial group is required for authenticity;

- where the job involves the provision of **personal services** to a particular racial group in order to promote their welfare and those services can be best provided by someone from the same racial group.

Sexual orientation

It is unlawful for employers to advertise vacancies, select interview candidates or offer employment in a way that discriminates on the ground of sexual orientation. Sexual orientation means orientation towards persons of the same sex, opposite sex and both sexes. In other words, it will cover homosexuals, heterosexuals and bisexuals.

As with sex and race discrimination, there are some jobs for which the sexual orientation of the candidate may be a genuine occupational qualification.

Religion or belief

It is unlawful for employers to advertise vacancies, select interview candidates or offer employment in any way that discriminates on the grounds of religion or belief.

As with sex and race discrimination there are some jobs for which the religion or belief of the candidate may be a genuine occupational qualification.

Age discrimination

There is currently no express legislation prohibiting discrimination on the ground of age, but there is a voluntary code of practice which attempts to tackle the problem of age discrimination. The government has announced proposals to introduce laws to stop age discrimination, which are due to be implemented by December 2006. Also see chapter 5 on age discrimination as unlawful indirect discrimination.

Trade unions

It is unlawful for an employer to refuse employment on the grounds of membership or non-membership of a trade union.

Pregnancy

In relation to pregnancy, any decision not to appoint a woman on the ground that she is pregnant is likely to be found to be discriminatory against sex.

Disability discrimination

It is unlawful for an employer to discriminate unjustifiably against a disabled person on the ground of disability. This law applies in a similar way to the current sex and race legislation at all stages in the recruitment process.

Employees' past criminal convictions

Spent convictions

After a certain period of time, people who have been convicted of criminal offences and who have served their sentences are not under a duty to disclose those convictions to a prospective employer. These convictions are known as 'spent' convictions. If spent convictions are disclosed to prospective employers, it is unlawful for them to take the offences into account when considering someone for a job and if they do so, they will be guilty of unlawful discrimination. The periods of time (known as 'rehabilitation periods') depend on the seriousness of the offence and are set out in Appendix 1. In certain professions, offices and occupations all previous offences must be disclosed regardless of the period of time that has expired.

Unspent convictions

In England & Wales (not Scotland), it is possible to check the criminal records of potential employees with the Criminal Records Bureau. Further details are available on the Criminal Records Bureau's website at www.crb.gov.uk or on 0870 909 0811.

Employing children and young persons

A 'child' is defined as anyone younger than the minimum school leaving age. 'Young persons' are defined as anyone over school leaving age but under 18. Young persons are protected by the Working Time Regulations, which limit the number of hours young workers may work and provide rules on the daily and weekly rest periods an employer must give to young workers.

No child may be employed:

- if under the age of 13 years;
- during school hours;
- before 7am or after 7pm;
- for more than two hours on any day on which he is required to attend school;
- for more than two hours on a Sunday;
- in any industrial undertaking; or
- where he is likely to suffer injury from lifting, carrying or moving heavy items.

A local education authority has powers to supervise the employment of school children in its area and may require particulars about a child's employment. It may prohibit or restrict employment if it feels that the employment is unsuitable, even if not unlawful. Therefore, an employer is advised to seek advice from its local education authority if it is considering employing a child. In order to employ a child an employer must also obtain a permit from the local education authority.

In addition, the Health and Safety Executive (HSE) provides guidance on the employment of younger workers. In particular, in December 2001 the HSE published guidance (*Catering Information Sheet CIS21*) on employers' legal duties for employing young people and children in catering.

Restrictions on employing women

The following restrictions on the employment of women are for the protection of women and it is lawful to discriminate in employment to comply with these requirements:

- employment in factories within four weeks of childbirth;

- employment in a range of processes involving lead or lead compounds;

- employment in a range of processes in the pottery industry;

- protection from exposure to ionising radiation; and

- employment on ships or aeroplanes while pregnant.

Employment of EU and EEA nationals

The member states of the European Union (EU) are: Austria, Belgium, Cyprus, the Czech Republic, Denmark, Estonia, Finland, France, Germany, Greece, Hungary, Ireland, Italy, Latvia, Lithuania, Luxembourg, Malta, the Netherlands, Poland, Portugal, Slovakia, Slovenia, Spain, Sweden and the United Kingdom. The European Economic Area (EEA) comprises EU members plus Iceland, Liechtenstein and Norway.

Citizens of the EU and EEA are known as European Nationals and they do not need work permits; they have the right to come to the UK and look for work. Family members of European Nationals also have an automatic right to accompany such European Nationals to the UK. However, if they wish to stay in the UK for more than six months, they are advised to apply for a residence permit.

Exception

Member states of the EU are entitled to exclude employment in public service from the general requirements of free movement of labour, and may reserve such employment for their own nationals. The definition of employment in public service in this context is not a question of status of the employee, but rather on whether the employee exercises powers conferred by public law or is responsible for safeguarding the general interests of the state.

Employment of non-EU nationals

Someone who is subject to immigration control must obtain a work permit before taking up employment in the UK, unless he belongs to one of the categories of people for whom this is not necessary. These include:

- ministers of religion;
- representatives of overseas newspapers, news agencies and broadcasting organisations;
- private servants of diplomatic staff;
- sole representatives of overseas firms;
- teachers and language assistants under approved exchange schemes;
- employees of an overseas government or international organisation;
- seamen under contract to join a ship in British waters;
- operational ground staff of overseas owned airlines;
- seasonal workers at agricultural camps under approved schemes;
- doctors and dentists in post-graduate training;
- business visitors admitted by the Home Office;
- Commonwealth citizens with the right of abode and those with at least one grandparent born in the UK.

For further details about applications for work permits, contact the Work Permits UK Helpline, listed in Appendix 32.

The Asylum and Immigration Act has been introduced to discourage illegal working in the UK. This creates a criminal offence (punishable by a fine of up to £5,000) of employing a person without immigration authorisation to work in the UK. An employer will have a defence if it can prove that it saw an original of one of a number of specified documents which confirmed that the employee was entitled to work in the UK (see Appendix 2). The Act is not retrospective so employers do not have to check the documentation of staff employed prior to January 1997. It is important for employers to adopt procedures which will protect them from prosecution but which also do not breach the race discrimination legislation (see chapter 5). The Home Office has published guidance notes for employers which are available by telephoning 0845 010 6677.

Recruitment guidelines

As well as complying with employment legislation, employers are encouraged to follow good practice when recruiting. The Equal Opportunities Commission, the Commission for Racial Equality and the Disability Rights Commission publish codes of practice and recruitment guidelines for employers. Failure to observe these codes of practice does not render an employer liable to proceedings. But, if proceedings are brought in an employment tribunal, any relevant provision of the codes may be taken into account. Employers are advised to consider their practices carefully at each stage in the recruitment process. These are divided into:

- Advertising

- Selecting and interviewing job applicants

- Choosing the successful candidate

- Making the job offer

Advertising

Employers must avoid biased language in recruitment advertising. Adverts will be illegal if they discourage certain groups (as identified in the discrimination section of this chapter) from applying. For example:

'Salesman wanted ...'

This is an example of gender bias because the word 'man' indicates that women applicants will not be considered for the position. The word 'salesperson' would be acceptable or, alternatively, an indication in the advertisement that both men and women may apply.

'Single professional sought ...'

This is an example of discrimination on the ground of marital status and is illegal because the employer is denying applications from qualified married people in favour of those who are unmarried.

In addition to the wording of the adverts, other points to consider, which the codes of practice referred to above recommend, are as follows:

- Always place adverts in publications or areas that are likely to reach both men and women and which do not exclude or proportionately reduce the number of applicants of a particular racial group.
- Never present men and women in stereotyped roles.
- Be wary of recruiting solely by word of mouth as this may limit members of a certain sex or race from applying.
- If applicants are supplied through trade unions and members of only one sex or a particular racial group (or a disproportionately high number of them) come forward, discuss this with the unions; an alternative approach may have to be adopted.
- Never make the length of residence in, or experience of, the UK a requirement of the job.
- If a qualification for the job is required, always state that a fully comparable overseas qualification is as acceptable as a UK one.

What should an advertisement include?

It is good practice to prepare a written description for each job title. From this written description, an employer may specify the most important duties and requirements of the vacant post in the advertisement as follows:

- The qualifications and experience required.
- Any specific skills required.
- Experience with specific equipment required.
- The salary and benefits offered.
- The person to contact.

- The required references.

If there is doubt about whether the advert is appropriate, ask the personnel department, a legal adviser or someone in a senior position to review it before it is published.

Selecting and interviewing job applicants

Selection criteria and/or tests

The purpose of selection criteria and tests is to ensure that an individual has the ability to perform or train for a particular job. The employer should avoid insisting on irrelevant qualifications. Selection criteria and tests should be reviewed regularly to ensure that they remain relevant and are not unlawfully discriminatory.

Once the selection of the applicants has been carried out, letters should be sent inviting candidates for interview and rejecting unsuccessful applicants (see the example letters at Appendices 3 and 4).

'Dos' and 'Don'ts' when selecting and interviewing job applicants

The following checklist outlines what the employer should and should not do during the selection and interview process:

Do

- process all applications in the same way;
- ask questions at the interview which relate to the requirements of the job;
- ensure that all employees who come into contact with job applicants are properly trained about the legal obligations in respect of discrimination and how to avoid unlawful discrimination;
- keep records of interviews showing why the applicants were or were not appointed.

Don't

- keep separate lists of male and female or married and single applicants;

- ask questions at the interview about personal circumstances such as marital status, children, domestic obligations, marriage plans or family intentions;

- make jokes at the interview that are sexist or racist or otherwise biased.

Suggested questions for a job applicant to ask at an employment interview

An employer should provide basic information about the employment contract during the interview. If the employer does not provide information that answers the following questions, the applicant should ask:

1. What is the nature of the job? What are the duties and responsibilities?

2. What is the wage for the job? When and how are wages paid? If wages and bonuses are negotiable, they should be discussed during the interview (a fair employer should answer these questions, although many recruitment agencies advise applicants to delay asking about salary and benefits until they have received a job offer. Also an employer's written job description often includes these details.).

3. What are the hours of work? Starting times, break times and finishing times should be explained. Is overtime paid at a higher rate? Can it be made part of the employment contract?

4. What is the holiday entitlement? If an employee works on bank holidays, is it compensated by overtime pay or time off on another day? Can unused holiday be carried over to the next year? Does an employee accrue holiday entitlement or holiday pay during maternity leave? Are employees paid accrued holiday pay if they leave the job?

5. What are the notice arrangements?

6. What are the sick pay arrangements?

7. What about pensions?

8. What is the disciplinary and grievance procedure?

While reading this book, prospective employees should make a note of any other issues that seem important. Employers respect applicants who prepare for the interview in advance and ask clear, well-framed questions.

Making the job offer

After the selection process, and once a suitable candidate has been chosen, a conditional offer should be made. References should then be taken up and medical examinations should be arranged if required (see the example letters at Appendices 5 and 6). Once the preferred candidate has accepted the offer, rejection letters should be sent to the unsuccessful candidates (see the example letter at Appendix 7). Where a candidate accepts a job offer, but subsequently changes his mind (possibly opting for another offer), this technically may be breach of contract; unless the employer can prove financial loss as a direct result, there is little that can be done.

CHAPTER 2

The employment relationship

The contract of employment is the legal basis of the employee/employer relationship. This chapter outlines the main principles of employment contracts which employers need to know in order to avoid legal problems. Employees also have a number of statutory rights which are also outlined in this chapter. Employees should also be aware of these so that they know their rights. The issues covered in this chapter are:

- General principles

- Statutory rights of employees

- Types of contracts of employment

- Terms of contract

- Variation of contract

- Staff Handbook

- Employees and the self-employed

General principles

A contract of employment is generally governed by the same legal principles as any other contract, in that there must be:

- an offer;

- an acceptance;

- valuable consideration;

- reasonable certainty in the terms; and

- an intention to create legal relations.

The contract may be oral or in writing or a mixture of the two and is governed by express and implied terms which set out the rights and obligations of the parties (see page 32). However, employers have a duty to issue their employees a written statement of the main terms and conditions under which they are to be employed. This must be issued within two months after the employment begins, but does not constitute the contract of employment. It is merely the employer's version of what it believes the main terms to be. The written statement may become a contract of employment, but only where the parties have expressly agreed to this. A mere signature by the employee to acknowledge receipt of the written statement does not amount to an agreement that the terms are the contract of employment.

In addition to the right to have a written statement issued, employees have further statutory rights, details of which follow. Subject to these statutory rights, the parties to a contract of employment are free to agree upon any terms they wish.

Statutory rights of employees

An employee becomes entitled to statutory rights (i.e. laid down by law) upon entering into an employment contract without any need for the details of these rights to be written into the contract. A number of these rights depend upon the employee having attained a qualifying period of employment. The main rights are described in more detail below.

1. **Equal opportunities** (see chapter 5)

2. **Itemised pay statements**

   An itemised pay statement must be issued to all employees at the time of payment and must include the following particulars:

   - Gross earnings.

- Net pay.

- Fixed and variable deductions from gross earnings.

- If the net pay is paid in different ways, the amount and method of payment of each part payment.

Employees may raise a complaint with an employment tribunal if the employer fails to issue a pay statement or if the content is in dispute.

3. **Equal pay for like work or work rated as equivalent or work of equal value** (see chapter 5)

4. **Maternity rights and benefits** (see chapter 3)

5. **Notice of termination of employment**

    Statute lays down minimum notice periods for termination of employment as follows:

    By the employer:

Length of service	Minimum notice period
Less than 1 month	Nil
1 month–2 years	1 week
2–3 years	2 weeks

and an additional week for each year of continuous employment to a maximum of 12 weeks.

By the employee: one week.

The contract of employment may impose a duty to give a longer period of notice.

See chapter 6 for further details on the recommended procedure for giving notice of termination of employment.

6. **Guarantee pay**

    'Guarantee' payments must be made to employees with at least one month's service, when they could normally expect to work but no work is available. Periods when employees are laid off because there is no work available must be agreed in advance to avoid the employer being in breach of contract.

An employee is entitled to a maximum payment of £18.40 per day for up to five days in any period of three months where he is laid off. Therefore, the annual maximum is currently £368. See Appendix 15 for an example notice to employees being laid off giving guarantee payments.

An employee may raise a complaint with an employment tribunal if his employer fails to pay the whole or part of a guarantee payment to which he is entitled. The employment tribunal can award compensation equal to the amount of the guarantee payment which it finds due to the employee.

7.   Redundancy pay (see chapter 6)

8.   Healthy and safe working environment

All employees are entitled to be provided by their employer 'so far as is reasonably practicable' with a safe place to work and access to the place of work, a safe system of work, adequate materials, competent fellow employees and protection from unnecessary risk of injury. Where there are more than five employees employed at any one time, the employer must prepare and bring to the notice of its employees a written statement of its policy with respect to health and safety at work.

A model policy, intended for smaller businesses, is available from The Stationery Office (www.tso.co.uk), but ideally the content of the policy statement should be tailored to meet the employer's particular requirements.

The Health and Safety at Work legislation is too complex to cover in this book, but employers should be aware of the importance of fulfilling their obligations. The Health and Safety Commission (HSC) and the Health and Safety Executive (HSE) are both established by the Health and Safety at Work etc Act 1974 and can provide advice. HSE publishes guidance notes on this subject which are available from HSE Books, listed at Appendix 32.

The Working Time Regulations provide for an average 48-hour working week, in-work rest breaks and 11 consecutive hours' rest in any 24-hour period, four weeks' paid holiday and an average eight hours' work in 24 hours for night workers. This means that employees are prevented from working any overtime which would result in their average working week exceeding 48 hours. However, the

Regulations enable individual employees to 'opt-out' and work in excess of this 48-hour limit. Any agreement to opt-out of this 48-hour limit must be in writing and a model opt-out agreement is provided at Appendix 12.

9. **Sickness benefit** (see chapter 4)

10. **Remuneration on suspension on medical grounds**

An employee is entitled to be paid for up to 26 weeks if he is suspended on medical grounds in compliance with any regulation or law which concerns the health and safety of workers.

An employee is only entitled to claim a medical suspension payment if he has been continuously employed for a period of one month. An employee employed for a fixed term of three months or less or under a specific task contract which is not expected to last for more than three months is not entitled to a medical suspension payment.

An employee will lose the right to payment where:

- he is incapable of work by reason of disease or bodily or mental disablement;

- the employer offered the employee suitable alternative employment (whether or not it was work that the employee was engaged to perform) and the employee unreasonably refused to perform that work; or

- he failed to comply with the employer's reasonable requirements imposed with a view to ensuring his services were available.

The amount an employee is entitled to be paid is 'a week's pay' (or a proportion of 'a week's pay') for every week of suspension. 'A week's pay' is calculated according to statutory rules and is also the basis for the calculation of redundancy payments and the basic award compensation for unfair dismissal. For an explanation of how to calculate a week's pay see the Department of Trade and Industry's booklet entitled *Rules Governing Continuous Employment and a Week's Pay*.

Employees may raise a complaint with an employment tribunal for failure to make a medical suspension payment. Such a complaint must be made within three months of the day on which it is alleged that payment was not made. The tribunal will extend the time limit if it was not reasonably practicable for the claim to be made within three months.

11. Time off

(a) Holiday

All workers have the right to the minimum of 20 days' paid holiday per year. Paid public holidays (of which there are eight in the UK) can be counted as part of the statutory 20 days' holiday entitlement. Some employers provide more generous contractual holiday entitlement than the statutory minimum.

Part-time workers are entitled to the same holidays as full-time workers, calculated on a pro rata basis. So, for example, where an employer gives full-time employees 20 days' holiday per year (plus public holidays), it should give an employee who works three days a week (Tuesday to Thursday) 12 days' paid holiday (plus 3/5 of the year's public holidays even if the part-timer does not work on Mondays).

The legislation does not entitle workers to carry leave over into the following year, nor may they receive payment in lieu to replace unused leave, except where the employment is terminated. The reason for this is to ensure that employees take holidays as a health and safety measure. It is not uncommon for contracts of employment to allow some holiday to be carried over or to attract payment in lieu; this is acceptable provided it is holiday that exceeds the statutory minimum of 20 days including public holidays.

Workers are entitled to a week's pay for each week of their statutory leave entitlement. This is relatively easy to calculate if the worker's pay does not vary with the amount of work done. However, if a worker's pay varies with the amount of work done or he is a shift or rota worker or if he has no normal working hours, then the amount of a week's pay is the average pay received over the preceding 12 weeks.

Generally, it is advisable for the employer to set out in the contract how a worker should apply for leave and how to seek approval before leave can be taken.

(b) Public duties

An employee is entitled to reasonable time off for the purpose of performing his public duties; see Appendix 16 for a full list of such duties.

There is no obligation to pay an employee when he takes time off for public duties. The amount of time off depends upon the employer's business and the effect of the employee's absence.

There is no statutory right to have time off for jury service or to attend court as a witness. However, an employer who prevents such attendance would be in contempt of court.

Although there is no legal obligation on employers to pay employees while they are on jury service, doing so is conducive to good employee relations. Jurors may, however, claim an allowance for travelling subsistence and financial loss.

(c) Trade union activities, duties and training

Officials of independent trade unions are entitled to time off with pay to perform duties concerned with the industrial relations in the company and to undergo training. There is also a right to time off to accompany another worker at disciplinary and grievance hearings.

Union members are entitled to time off without pay in order to take part in trade union activities.

(d) Elected employee representatives

An employee who has been elected for consultation purposes for collective redundancies or the transfer of an undertaking is entitled to reasonable paid time off to perform the functions of a representative. He also has the right to paid time off to undergo training.

(e) Safety representatives

Safety representatives who have been appointed by recognised trade unions are entitled to paid time off during working time to carry out their functions and undergo training in aspects of these functions. Representatives of non-unionised workplaces are also entitled to paid time off to carry out their functions and undergo training.

(f) Pension scheme trustees

Pension scheme trustees of the employer's own scheme are entitled to time off during working hours for performing the duties as a trustee or for training in connection with those duties.

(g) Maternity leave, including antenatal care or adoption leave (see chapter 3)

(h) Redundancy

An employee who is declared redundant and has at least two years' continuity of employment is entitled to reasonable, paid time off to look for a new job or to arrange training for a new job.

An employee may raise a complaint with an employment tribunal if the employer refuses to allow such time off or fails to pay for it.

(i) Parental leave

Both men and women are entitled to take up to 13 weeks' unpaid leave from work for the purpose of caring for a child for whom they have responsibility. For full details see chapter 3.

(j) Paternity leave

Employees have a right to take up to two weeks' paternity leave in connection with the birth or adoption of a child, where the child has been born or placed for adoption on or after 6 April 2003; for full details see chapter 3.

(k) Time off for dependants

There is also a right for employees to take a reasonable amount of unpaid leave to deal with incidents involving dependants; for full details see chapter 3.

12. Protected rights on the transfer of a trade or business

Where a trade or business is transferred from one employer to another, the employees of that trade or business automatically become employees of the new employer, as if their contract of employment were originally made with the new employer. The service is counted as continuous from the date on which the employment commenced with the first employer.

It is beyond the scope of this book to cover fully this complex area of employment law, and those who think they may be involved in a transfer of a trade or business should seek professional advice.

13. Not to be unfairly dismissed (see chapter 6)

14. Written reasons for dismissal (upon request)

An employee does not have an automatic right to a written statement of reasons for dismissal. However, if the employee has one year's continuous service and asks his employer for such a statement, the employer must provide one (the rules for assessing what is continuous service are set out in sections 210 to 219 of the Employment Rights Act 1996).

In practice, it is a good idea to give the dismissed employee the reasons for dismissal in the notice of termination.

15. Written statement of terms and conditions of employment

All employees have a right to be provided with a written statement of the terms and conditions of their employment, unless their employment is for a period of less than one month.

The information that the employer provides may be given in instalments, but certain items must be given in a single document, described as the *principal statement* (see Appendix 9). Reference to other documents is permitted only in relation to certain limited matters. As already mentioned, the principal statement does not automatically constitute a contract of employment, even if the employee acknowledges receipt of it with his signature. To be enforceable, the parties must expressly agree that it is the contract of employment. It is quite usual for the particulars, which constitute the written statement of terms and conditions, to be incorporated into the contract of employment, so that a separate document does not then have to be issued to the employee. The model contract of employment in this book at Appendix 11 incorporates all the particulars that must be included in the principal statement.

An employee employed for more than 13 weeks may raise a complaint with an employment tribunal if his employer fails to provide the written statement of the terms of employment. If a statement has been given but a question arises about particulars that should have been included in it, either the employee or employer may apply to an employment tribunal.

16. Minimum wage

An employee's rate of pay must not be below the National Minimum Wage (NMW) which is currently £4.85 per hour (increasing to £5.05 on 1 October 2005, and to £5.35 on 1 October 2006) before deductions for those aged 22 and above, £4.10 (increasing to £4.25 on 1 October 2005, and to £4.45 on 1 October 2006) for those aged 18–21 and those in the first six months of a new job doing specific training. People aged 16 and 17, those on formal apprenticeships and those working and living as part of a family are not entitled to the NMW. Claims for the NMW are heard in the employment tribunal. For more details contact the NMW Helpline on 0845 600 0678 or the DTI website at www.tiger.gov.uk.

17. Sunday shop working

A person employed as a shop worker, except those employed to work only on Sundays, has the right not to:

- be dismissed for refusing to work on Sundays;
- be selected for redundancy for refusing to work on Sundays;
- suffer any other detriment for refusing to work on Sundays.

There are provisions in the Sunday Trading Act 1994 entitling shop workers to opt-out of and into Sunday shop work. All shop workers who were employed on or before 26 August 1994, even those who had previously agreed to a contract requiring them to work on Sunday, and any shop workers recruited after that date whose contract of employment does not require Sunday working but whose employer asks them to work on Sundays, simply need to tell their employer that they do not wish to work on Sundays. Shop workers who entered into a contract requiring Sunday working after 26 August 1994, even those who had previously agreed to a contract requiring them to work on Sunday, and agreed to do shop work on Sundays can opt-out of Sunday working at any time, but they need to give their employer a written notice and then serve a three-month notice period; during the three-month notice period they will still be obliged to work Sundays if their contract provides for it and if their employer wants them to do it; the right not to work on Sundays applies as from the end of the three-month period.

Employers are required to give every shop worker who enters into a contractual agreement to work on Sundays a written explanatory statement setting out his right to opt-out. If an employer does not issue this statement within two months of the worker entering into such a contract arrangement, the opt-out notice period is reduced from three months to one month. The prescribed text of such an explanatory statement is set out in Appendix 13.

18. Access to Stakeholder Pensions

An employer of more than five full-time employees who have at least three months' service (including directors) is required to offer its employees access to Stakeholder Pensions, unless it already provides a pension scheme that meets certain criteria. Stakeholder Pensions are flexible, low cost and tax-effective retirement saving plans aimed at people earning over £10,000 a year who are not members of a company pension scheme. Stakeholder Pensions will not be compulsory for the employee.

It is beyond the scope of this book to cover fully the area of pensions law, but for further advice on the implementation and administration of Stakeholder Pensions contact the Pensions Advisory Service's Helpline on 0845 601 2923.

19. Statutory dispute resolution procedures

All employers are bound by statutory dispute resolution procedures. Employers are required to apply certain procedures when dealing with disciplinary or dismissal situations. Employees also have to take certain steps to try to resolve their grievances with their employer before bringing a claim in an employment tribunal.

Whenever an employer is contemplating dismissing an employee or taking disciplinary action other than giving a warning (e.g. demotion or transferring him to work in a different department) it must follow the standard dismissal and disciplinary procedure.

A modified procedure applies in cases where the employer has already dismissed the employee in circumstances in which it was reasonable to do so without investigating the circumstances (e.g. the employee has been violent in the workplace and poses a real threat to the employer). This will be very rare indeed, as even in this example in most cases the threat can be overcome by suspending the employee and then investigating the matter. Furthermore, it is always advisable to establish the facts and give the employee the opportunity to put his case at a disciplinary meeting before taking any action in order to ensure dismissal is not unfair. It is important to note that even if the employer complies with the correct statutory dispute resolution procedure, dismissal may still be unfair. For further details on unfair dismissal, see chapter 6. Therefore it is recommended that employers always adopt the standard dismissal and disciplinary procedure. For details of the standard and modified procedures, see Appendix 10.

Note: The standard procedure must be applied by employers for all dismissals, including those on non-disciplinary grounds (e.g. redundancy, expiry of a fixed-term contract or compulsory retirement).

The main consequence of a failure by an employer to follow the procedures is that dismissal will be deemed to be automatically unfair (subject to the employee having a year's service) and the compensatory award may be increased or decreased by between ten and 50 per cent, depending on which party is at fault (subject to the statutory cap of £56,800). For further details on unfair dismissal and automatically unfair dismissal, see chapter 6.

Where an employee has a grievance about an action by his employer, he will need to initiate the statutory grievance procedure (see Appendix 10) before he can bring a subsequent employment tribunal claim. It is recommended that whenever an employee raises a grievance (verbally or in writing) an employer follows the standard statutory grievance procedure. The modified procedure should only be applied after termination of employment and where both parties agree to follow this procedure.

Types of contract of employment

There are a number of different types of contract of employment. When deciding which is the most appropriate, the employer should consider the type of work, the duration of the employment and the nature of the employment relationship that is sought by both parties.

Contract for an indefinite period

The majority of contracts of employment are for an indefinite period, as is the model contract included in this book (see Appendix 11). They can be terminated by either party giving notice. The period of notice should be specified in the contract, but if not, there is an implied term (see page 32) that the contract may be terminated upon reasonable notice. In deciding what is reasonable, the following should be taken into account:

- The seniority of the employee.

- The remuneration of the employee.

- The age of the employee.

- The length of service of the employee.

- What is usual in the trade.

However, it is more advisable to express the notice period. To determine this, employers should consider the following:

- How long is it likely to take to find a replacement for the employee if he resigns?

- Will a replacement need to be trained?

- How much would it cost to make a payment in lieu of notice? Long notice periods can be very costly.

- Is it possible that the employee will work for or become a competitor? In these circumstances, a relatively long notice period is advisable.

- What is reasonable to expect from the employee?

- What is competitive in the market place?

The contractual notice period must not be less than the statutory minimum period of notice referred to on page 17, but if the contractual notice is longer, then the longer period must be given.

Fixed-term contracts

A fixed-term contract is one that has a termination date. The duration of the fixed-term contract may be for any period. Fixed-term contracts may provide that the notice to terminate can be given before the termination date. If there is no notice provision, employment is guaranteed for the full period.

A fixed-term contract will automatically expire at the end of its term. Failure to renew a fixed-term contract upon termination may lead to a valid claim for unfair dismissal or redundancy pay (see page 111).

Fixed-term employees may complain to an employment tribunal about any objectively unjustifiable less favourable treatment accorded to them by their employer and compared to that accorded to a comparable permanent employee on the ground of their fixed-term status. A comparable permanent employee is one who is engaged in broadly similar work with a similar level of qualification, skill and experience and who is employed by the same employer.

Broadly, in order to comply with the obligations toward fixed-term employees, unless the employer has a genuine business need to do otherwise, it should ensure that:

- fixed-term employees receive the same hourly rate and overtime rate as comparable permanent employees;

- fixed-term employees are not treated less favourably than comparable permanent employees in terms of: the rate of any contractual sick or maternity pay, the length of service required to qualify for payment; the length of time the payment is received; and their holiday entitlement, bonus entitlement or other contractual benefits;

- it does not discriminate between fixed-term employees over access to pension schemes;

- it does not exclude fixed-term employees from training simply because they are on a fixed-term contract;

- contractual maternity leave, parental leave, adoption leave and paternity leave are available to fixed-term employees as well as to comparable permanent employees;

- career break schemes are available to fixed-term employees and comparable permanent employees in the same way;

- the criteria used to select jobs for redundancy are objectively justified, and fixed-term employees are not less favourably treated than comparable permanent employees.

The use of successive fixed-term contracts is limited to a maximum of four years (starting from 1 October 2002) unless their use for a longer period can be justified. Any contracts continuing beyond this four-year period shall be deemed to be permanent contracts.

Fixed-term employees also have the right to be informed by their employer of all available permanent vacancies in the business. This can be achieved by posting all vacancies on internal notice boards.

Fixed-term employees also have anti-victimisation rights. Any dismissal of a fixed-term employee because he has exercised any right under the Fixed-Term Employees (Prevention of Less Favourable Treatment) Regulations 2002 is automatically unfair, regardless of the employee's length of service or whether the employee is above normal retiring age. Such employees also have the right not to suffer any detriment short of dismissal on the ground of that action.

Contracts for specific tasks

Contracts for the completion of a specific task automatically terminate once the task is completed. They are also covered by the law protecting fixed-term employees (see above).

Short-term contracts

These can be used where the work to be done can be completed within a short period of time. Where the contract is for less than three months the employee is not entitled to statutory sick pay or medical suspension pay. However, if a second such contract is entered into with the same employer and it is continuous with the first, then the employer becomes liable to pay statutory sick pay or medical suspension pay.

Service contracts

This is the name given to a contract of employment for more senior employees. Service contracts may be fixed-term contracts renewable on a regular basis or they may be 'rolling' service contracts in which the contract continues after the expiry of a fixed period and then can only be terminated by not less than, say, one year's notice.

Although service contracts can be expensive for a company, they offer a measure of security and so are attractive for employees.

Directors may not have service contracts for more than five years without the agreement of the shareholders of the company at a general meeting.

Part-time contracts

An increasing number of employees are now engaged on a part-time basis. Such employees have the right not to be treated less favourably by their employers than a full-time co-worker with broadly similar qualifications, skills and experience, who is engaged in the same or broadly similar work.

Part-time workers may complain to an employment tribunal about any objectively unjustifiable less favourable treatment accorded to them by their employer and compared to that accorded to a relevant full-time worker on the ground of their part-time status. Note that workers, a broader category than employees, are protected by these rights. Broadly, in order to comply with the obligations toward the part-time worker, unless the employer has a genuine business need to do otherwise, it should ensure that:

- part-time workers receive the same hourly rate as comparable full-time employees;

- part-time workers receive hourly rates of overtime comparable to full-time rates, once they have worked more than the normal full-time hours;

- part-time workers are not treated less favourably than full-time employees in terms of: the rate of any contractual sick or maternity pay, the length of service required to qualify for payment, the length of time the payment is received, and their bonus entitlement or other contractual benefits;

- it does not discriminate between full-time employees and part-time workers over access to pension schemes; the calculation of benefits from the pension scheme for part-time staff should be on a pro rata basis as the calculation for full-time employees;

- it does not exclude part-time workers from training simply because they work part-time (although there is no legal obligation to plan the training to accommodate their schedules);

- the contractual holiday entitlement of part-time workers is pro rata that of full-time employees;

- contractual maternity leave, parental leave, adoption leave and paternity leave are available to part-time workers as well as to full-time employees;

- career break schemes are available to part-time workers and full-time employees in the same way;

- the criteria used to select jobs for redundancy are objectively justified, and part-time workers are not less favourably treated than comparable full-time employees.

Part-time workers also have anti-victimisation rights. Any dismissal of a part-time worker because he has exercised any right under the Part-Time Workers (Prevention of Less Favourable Treatment) Regulations 2000 is automatically unfair, regardless of the worker's length of service or whether the employee is above normal retiring age. Such workers also have the right not to suffer any detriment short of dismissal on the ground of that action.

Certain employees (both male and female) have had the right to request flexible working for the purpose of caring for a child and employers will have a legal duty to consider such applications – see chapter 3 for more details. In addition, employers should also bear in mind that inflexible working practices (such as a refusal to allow an employee to return from maternity leave to work part-time) may also be challenged as indirectly sex discriminatory.

Terms of contract

Express and implied terms

Usually, the parties to the contract will have expressly stated the major terms of the contract. These may be written or oral, but it is obviously preferable to put these terms in writing in order to minimise future disputes. Even though in practice express, oral terms may be just as binding as written ones, they are very much more difficult to prove.

In addition to the express terms of the contract, all contracts of employment have what is known as 'implied terms'.

Implied terms are not stated expressly in the contract because:

- they are too obvious to be recorded; or

- they are common practice within the particular business or industry and are precise, reasonable and well known; or

- they are necessary to make the contract work; or

- the parties to the contract have shown by their behaviour their acceptance of such terms.

A term is not implied simply because it would be reasonable to include it. There are terms which are accepted as commonly implied in employment contracts relating to the employer's and the employee's duties, as shown in the table opposite.

In addition to those in the table, terms may be implied into a contract of employment by legislation, for example, equality clauses which are implied by the Equal Pay Act 1970; these terms automatically apply to any contract.

Terms may also be incorporated into a contract of employment from other sources. Prime examples are terms which may be implied into an individual contract through collective agreements and work rules or Staff Handbooks.

Common implied terms

Employer's duties

- to pay wages

- to co-operate with the employee and maintain mutual trust and confidence

- to take reasonable care for the health and safety of the employee

- to take reasonable steps to bring to the employee's attention any contractual rights which are dependent on him taking action, but which the employee may be reasonably unaware of

- to exercise pension rights in good faith

- to deal reasonably and promptly with employees' grievances

- to give a reasonable period of notice of termination when no specific period of notice has been agreed

Employee's duties

- to work for the employer with due diligence and care

- to co-operate with the employer, including obeying lawful orders, and maintain trust and confidence and not impede the employer's business

- to follow a duty of fidelity, i.e. not compete with the employer and not disclose confidential information unless it is in the public interest

- to take reasonable care for his own safety and that of fellow employees

- to give a reasonable period of notice of termination when no specific period of notice has been agreed

Unenforceable terms

1. Unlawful terms or terms contrary to public policy

For example, a contract which has the effect of being a fraud on the Inland Revenue or a contract under which a foreign employee works illegally without a work permit.

2. **Terms purporting to contract out of employment protection legislation**

3. **Discriminatory terms**

   For example, on the grounds of sex, race or disability.

4. **Terms in restraint of trade if their main purpose is to restrain competition**

   Such terms *are* enforceable, however, if their main purpose is to protect something in which the employer has a legitimate business interest worthy of protection. For any such clause to be enforceable, it needs to be carefully drafted, taking into account the nature of the employee's work. If the clause is too wide, it will be void. The courts will not rewrite clauses to make them enforceable; an example of a restraint of trade clause is given at clause 10 at Appendix 11.

5. **Terms which purport to exclude or restrict liability for death or personal injury resulting from negligence**

   In the case of loss or damage other than death or personal injury a contract term may only exclude or restrict liability for negligence if it satisfies the requirement of reasonableness (for further details on this, see the Unfair Contract Terms Act 1977).

Variation of contract

An employer does not have an automatic right to vary an employee's terms of employment. The extent to which employers can unilaterally change an employee's terms or working arrangements will depend entirely on the terms themselves.

Existing terms

Flexibility may be expressly built into the contract by, for example, the inclusion of wide terms or narrow, but changeable, terms. An example of the former is, 'You may be required to work anywhere in the UK', while an example of the latter is, 'You will work eight hours in 24, day, night or shift work'. Another way flexibility may have been built into the contract is by the use of terms which can be altered in content or removed. For example, a bonus may be stated to be payable at the manager's discretion.

The contract may also contain what is known as 'machinery for change'. For example, the Staff Handbook 'as issued from time to time' may be stated to be incorporated. This would mean that matters dealt with in the Handbook could be changed and the change incorporated into the contract, without the need of the employee's express consent.

If the contract contains such flexible clauses or incorporates machinery for change, then the employer will be able to alter the terms in line with these clauses provided the implementation of such alterations is carried out in a reasonable manner; for example, if a mobility clause is included in the contract, the employer should give reasonable notice before requiring an employee to relocate.

If there is no flexibility or machinery for change, then employers must follow the correct procedure if they want to alter an employee's terms of employment in order to minimise the possibility of claims for damages and/or compensation relating to the change.

Offering new terms to the employee

The first step for the employer is to offer the new terms to the employee. He can either accept or reject them. Acceptance must be positive, unequivocal and unconditional. There is no particular form of offering or acceptance required, so it can be oral, written or by conduct. Appendix 17 provides an example letter from an employer to an employee altering the terms of employment. However, by doing nothing, it cannot be said that an employee has accepted the new terms. The only time doing nothing can amount to acceptance is when the contract contains a term making this so. An example of such a term would be, 'If you do not object in writing within 14 days you will be deemed to have accepted the change'. It is possible for an employee to accept the new terms by his conduct: if he changes his behaviour to comply with a term in the offer (e.g. he turns up for work at a new time) he will be taken to have accepted the new terms.

Dismiss and offer employment on new terms

If the employee does not accept the changes, the only other option for the employer is to dismiss him and offer employment on the new terms. However, by doing this, the employer may become liable for claims for breach of contract, unfair dismissal or redundancy if the correct procedures are not followed and the appropriate reasons for dismissal do not exist. Termination of employment is dealt with in greater detail in chapter 6, but if employers wish to take this route it is suggested that they take advice before doing so.

Staff Handbook

An employer will always have a number of practices and procedures that it will want to apply to its employees. Generally, it is advisable for these to be contained in one document, which should be issued to all employees at the commencement of their employment. Employees should be asked to confirm that they have read and understood the Staff Handbook.

However, it is also important for the employer to retain the ability to amend the practices and procedures in the Staff Handbook, and therefore the statement, 'the Staff Handbook, as amended from time to time, applies to all employees' should be put in the introduction. The Staff Handbook should also be referred to in the contract (see clause 14 of Appendix 11).

The Staff Handbook may contain a variety of procedures and will vary from employer to employer, but in nearly all cases it should include the following:

- Equal Opportunities Policy
- Disciplinary Rules and Procedures
- Grievance Procedure
- Health and Safety Policy

A model Staff Handbook is shown at Appendix 14 which includes examples of matters that an employer may wish to include in a Staff Handbook and may be adapted according to the employer's needs and requirements. It is beyond the scope of this book to cover all administrative issues that may need to be included in a Staff Handbook, so it is important that an employer considers its own needs and requirements when preparing its own Staff Handbook.

Use of telephones, email and the internet

Because of the way in which people's work has changed, with the growth of email, voicemail and other office-based communications, there has been an increase in an employer's need to control the use of and monitor such communications. It is essential for an employer to be clear with the employees the extent to which it will tolerate the use of these business tools for personal use. Not only does this reduce the likelihood of employees overusing the telephone, email and internet and spending less time carrying out their duties, but also if they do abuse the system, the employer is in a stronger position to take disciplinary action against the employee because it can point to a clear procedure which has been violated.

There are a variety of reasons why an employer may wish to have the right to monitor email or telephone calls, such as a need to open the email of an employee who is on holiday, the need to monitor performance or unauthorised use or, in particular, the use of offensive material or the detection of damaging computer viruses.

Recent law entitles employers to intercept certain types of communications in defined circumstances, without the consent of the sender or the recipient, where the interception is only for the purpose of monitoring or keeping a record of communications relevant to the business in question. The defined circumstances where such interception is authorised are:

- to establish the existence of facts relevant to the business (e.g. where it may be necessary to know specific facts of a conversation);

- to check that the company is complying with external regulatory or internal regulatory rules or guidelines;

- to ascertain or demonstrate standards which are, or ought to be, achieved by persons using the system (e.g. for the purposes of staff training or quality control);

- to prevent or detect crime (e.g. to detect fraud);

- to investigate or detect the unauthorised use of telecommunications systems (e.g. to ensure employees do not breach company rules or policies on the use of the email system or the internet);

- to ensure the effective operation of the system (e.g. monitoring for viruses).

An employer is also entitled to monitor, but not record without consent, in order:

- to determine whether or not the communications are relevant to the business (e.g. where a member of staff is on holiday or off sick, it may be necessary to access his emails to determine whether they are relevant to the business);

- to monitor communications to confidential, anonymous, counselling or support helplines. This includes the monitoring of calls to confidential helplines to protect or support helpline staff.

While this law authorises the monitoring or recording of a wide range of communications, such information is likely to be covered by the data protection principles contained in the Data Protection Act 1998 and therefore must be processed in a way that does not violate those principles. The Office of the Information Commissioner has issued a code of practice that deals with the question of email and telephone monitoring. Broadly, employers must only monitor after first establishing that there is a problem that calls for monitoring. In respect of email, the employer should carry out traffic monitoring to determine whether the system is being abused and, in relation to telephone monitoring, an itemised call record may be an appropriate initial step. The code makes it clear that there should only be monitoring where there is a real business need and the methods used to carry it out should be proportionate and not unduly intrusive into the individual's privacy. Accordingly, employers should be very careful in exercising their right to monitor under this legislation.

Employees and the self-employed

This chapter has so far dealt with the employment relationship, i.e. between an employer and employee. However, any person who works for another person or organisation in return for remuneration has a contractual relationship with him or it, but it may be as a consultant or a self-employed person. There is an extremely important distinction between an employee and a self-employed person because their legal rights differ in a number of ways.

A contract of employment (sometimes referred to as a *contract of service*) is the name given to the agreement an employee has with an employer. A contract for services is the name given to the agreement between a self-employed person (or independent sub-contractor) and the person or organisation to whom he is providing the services.

To distinguish between a contract of employment and a contract for services it is necessary to look at the reality of the relationship, not merely the name of the agreement.

How to distinguish a contract of employment from a contract for services

Questions to consider in determining whether a person is an employee or is self-employed are:

1. Are there mutual obligations on the employer to provide work for the person engaged and on the person engaged to perform work for the employer?

2. Is he performing services for other people as a person in business on his own account?

3. Is he working under the orders of the person to whom he is supplying the services who controls when, how and what he must do?

4. Does he provide his own machinery and equipment?

5. Does he hire his own helpers?

6. Does he take a degree of financial risk?

7. Is the engagement for a specific, finite project or does it carry a degree of responsibility for ongoing administration or management?

8. Does he have the possibility of profiting from sound management in the performance of his tasks?

The greater degree of personal responsibility the person engaged undertakes in any of the above, the more likely he is to be considered self-employed rather than an employee. Other factors may include the method of payment, the method of paying tax and National Insurance, payment during absence for illness or for holidays, membership of company pension schemes and a prohibition on working for other companies or individuals.

Although the above questions are relevant considerations, they will not be appropriate in every case and the answer to the question is not found by merely using these questions as a checklist. It is important to assess each case individually.

If there is any doubt as to the nature of the relationship, the parties may agree on what the legal situation between them is to be. However, it will not be conclusive when questions of tax, social security or statutory employment protection arise. If the matter goes to a court or tribunal, all the circumstances will be considered to ascertain the true nature of the relationship.

To add to the confusion, some of the more recent legislation (such as the Working Time Regulations) replaces the term 'employee' with the term 'worker'. A worker includes both employees and others who provide services personally (although not under a client relationship), but does not include a person who is genuinely self-employed. This greatly increases the number of people protected by such legislation.

Practical and legal implications

Employees' statutory rights were dealt with earlier in this chapter. The self-employed do not have these statutory rights, but here is a list of the rights and obligations they do have:

Rights of the self-employed

- Equal opportunities, i.e. non-discrimination on the grounds of race, sex, disability, sexual orientation and religion or belief.

- To be provided with a safe place of work and a safe system of work.

- To be paid wages or fees free of any deductions not properly authorised.

Obligations of the self-employed

- To work with due skill and diligence.

- To pay Income Tax under Schedule D.

- To pay self-employed person's National Insurance contributions.

- To fulfil contractual obligations.

The Inland Revenue has introduced rules to remove opportunities for the avoidance of tax and Class 1 National Insurance Contributions by the use of intermediaries, such as service companies or partnerships, in circumstances where the individual worker would otherwise be considered to be an employee. The new rules determine that, where workers meet the definition of employees in relation to work done for their clients, they will pay broadly the same tax and National Insurance contributions as an employee, even if they provide their services through an intermediary. For further details, please see the Inland Revenue website at www.inlandrevenue.gov.uk.

CHAPTER 3

Family-friendly rights

Employees have some important statutory rights in relation to their family responsibilities (subject, in some circumstances, to them satisfying certain qualifying conditions), which aim to strike a balance between their work and home commitments. This chapter describes the various rights and is divided into sections as follows:

- Maternity rights

- Adoption rights

- Parental leave

- Time off for dependants

- Paternity rights

- Right to request flexible working

Maternity rights

The main statutory rights that a female employee who is expecting a baby has are explained in this chapter and are as follows:

- Time off for antenatal care

- Protection from dismissal and detrimental treatment

- Suspension from work on maternity grounds

- The right to take maternity leave and return to work

- Statutory maternity pay

Time off for antenatal care

All pregnant employees are entitled to paid time off for antenatal care, irrespective of their length of service or the number of hours worked by them. This right applies only to pregnant women; husbands of pregnant women have no statutory right to attend antenatal appointments with their wives.

Except in the case of the first appointment, the employee must produce a certificate confirming her pregnancy and an appointment card or some other document showing that an appointment has been made, if requested to do so by her employer.

The actual length of absence for antenatal care must be reasonable. It may include time for travelling to and from an appointment. If an appointment lasts longer than expected, the employer should still be obliged to pay the employee for the whole of the time that was required to attend the appointment. However, employees must not abuse their right by taking more time off than is necessary.

It may be reasonable for an employer to refuse an employee time off. Such a refusal is reasonable in the circumstances that the employee can arrange to have the antenatal care outside normal working hours. Therefore, part-time staff or shift workers may be able to arrange appointments outside their normal working hours. However, the timing of appointments is often outside the individual's control and, if this is so, the employee should explain this to her employer. In these circumstances, it would be unreasonable for the employer to refuse the employee time off for antenatal care during her working hours. An employer cannot require an employee who takes time off for antenatal care to make up the time later.

What care is included in the right?

Statute does not define antenatal care except that it must be on the advice of a registered medical practitioner, midwife or health visitor. As a general guideline, however, it should be assumed that standard antenatal clinic visits are covered. The number of visits required and the length of each visit depends on the medical condition of the employee concerned.

An employment tribunal has held that exercise and relaxation classes also fall within the definition of antenatal care. But such classes would have to be on the recommendation of the employee's medical advisers.

There is no right to be paid for time off for infertility treatment. However, if an individual receiving infertility treatment becomes pregnant, then she enjoys the same statutory protection as any other pregnant employee. It is likely that she would need more time off work for antenatal care and an employer would be obliged to allow her the time off as it would probably be considered reasonable.

Doctors' appointments for the purpose of ascertaining whether or not an employee is pregnant would probably be regarded as antenatal care if the employee turned out to be pregnant, but if the employee were told that she was not pregnant, she would not be covered by the statutory right.

Pay entitlement

The employee should be paid her normal hourly rate of pay by her employer during the period of time off. If the employee is paid on the basis of a fixed salary, she should be paid as usual. Where an employee is paid by the hours she works, the rate of pay is calculated by dividing the amount of one week's pay by the normal working hours in a week.

If the number of hours worked per week is irregular, they should be averaged over the previous 12 complete working weeks. If the employee has not been employed for 12 weeks, the average should be calculated on the number of normal working hours in a week which she could reasonably expect to work under her contract of employment, or from the number of hours worked by any fellow employees in comparable employment.

Some employees may have a contractual right to be paid for time off for antenatal care. There is no right to receive both contractual pay and statutory pay and such entitlements can be offset against each other.

Remedies

If an employee is unreasonably refused time off, she would be guilty of misconduct if she took the time off without authorisation. However, an employee may raise a complaint with an employment tribunal if:

- her employer unreasonably refuses to give her time off for antenatal care; or

- her employer fails to pay her the appropriate amount for the time taken off for the antenatal appointment.

If a complaint is upheld, the tribunal will make a declaration to that effect. Where the complaint is a refusal to allow time off, the tribunal will order that the employer pays the employee the amount of remuneration to which she would have been entitled had time off been allowed. Where the complaint is a failure to pay the whole or part of the amount due, the tribunal will order that the employer pays the amount due.

If an employer unreasonably refuses to allow an employee time off for antenatal care and she has at least one year's service, she may also claim constructive dismissal in an employment tribunal. It is automatically unfair to dismiss a woman on the ground that she took proceedings to enforce her right to time off for antenatal care or to allege that such a right had been infringed.

The right to time off for antenatal care should not be confused with time off for sickness during pregnancy.

Protection from dismissal and detrimental treatment

Dismissal or selection for redundancy of any woman who is pregnant, or has recently given birth, is automatically unfair regardless of her length of service or hours of work if any of the following apply:

- The reason or principal reason for dismissal is that she is pregnant or any other reason connected with her pregnancy.

- Her maternity leave period (as defined below) is ended by her dismissal and the reason or principal reason for her dismissal is that she has given birth to a child or any other reason connected with her having given birth to a child.

- The reason or principal reason for her dismissal, where her contract of employment was terminated at the end of her maternity leave period, is that she took, or otherwise availed herself of, the benefits of maternity leave.

- The reason or principal reason for her dismissal is a requirement or recommendation to suspend her on health and safety grounds.

- The reason or principal reason for her dismissal is that she has given birth to a child, or any other reason connected with her having given birth to a child, and her contract of employment was terminated within four weeks of the end of the maternity leave period. The circumstances of termination were such that she remained incapable of work by reason of disease or other disablement and there was in force at that time a certificate from a medical practitioner issued during the maternity leave period.

- The reason or principal reason for her dismissal is that she is redundant and her employer has not offered her suitable available alternative employment.

For further details on unfair dismissals and the remedies available for unfair dismissal, see chapter 6.

A dismissal by reason of pregnancy may also amount to direct discrimination on the ground of sex (see chapter 5).

Employees also have the right not to be subjected to detrimental treatment on the grounds of pregnancy, childbirth (where the detriment took place during the ordinary or additional maternity leave period) or maternity. No qualifying service is required and employees may seek redress through an employment tribunal for infringements of this right.

An employee who is dismissed at any time during her pregnancy or maternity period is entitled to written reasons for her dismissal, regardless of length of service, without having to make a request for written reasons. An employee may raise a complaint with an employment tribunal if she is not provided with written reasons for her dismissal. If the employment tribunal finds the employer has breached this obligation unreasonably, it may make a declaration as to what it finds the employer's reasons for dismissal to have been. The employment tribunal may also award the employee a sum equivalent to two weeks' pay.

Suspension from work on maternity grounds

Under health and safety at work legislation, employers have an obligation to carry out risk assessments for the safety of employees. This assessment must include any risk posed to the health and safety of a woman who is of childbearing age.

If the assessment shows that there is a risk to an employee, the employer has an obligation to take preventative or protective action. The employer may need to vary the employee's working conditions or hours of work. If this would not be reasonable or would not avoid the risk, the employee has a right to be offered any suitable alternative work which is available. If no suitable alternative work is available, the employer has a duty to suspend the employee from work for as long as necessary to avoid the risk. The employee has these rights regardless of length of service or the number of hours that she works. However, to be entitled to these rights the employee must notify her employer in writing that she is pregnant, has given birth within the previous six months or is breastfeeding. Sick notes, giving an indication of pregnancy, may amount to written notification for these purposes.

Right to suitable alternative work

Alternative work is only suitable if it is both convenient and appropriate for the employee in question and is on terms and conditions no less favourable than her normal terms and conditions.

If suitable alternative work is available but the employer fails to offer it to the employee, the employee may raise a complaint with an employment tribunal, which may award compensation.

If the employer makes an offer of suitable alternative work but the employee unreasonably refuses the offer, she loses her right to be paid remuneration for the period of suspension (as described below).

Remuneration during suspension

If an employee is suspended on maternity pay, she is entitled to full pay during the period of her suspension (subject to above). In addition to the statutory right, an employee may have a contractual right to remuneration during maternity suspension. In these circumstances, such entitlements should be offset against each other.

During the period of maternity suspension an employee retains her continuity of employment.

If an employer fails to pay an employee all or part of any money due, the employee may raise a complaint with an employment tribunal, which will award her the amount of remuneration that it finds due.

The right to take maternity leave and return to work

All employees who are expecting a baby are entitled to 26 weeks' ordinary maternity leave, regardless of their length of service or hours of work. Employees who are expecting a baby and have 26 weeks' continuous service with their employer by the beginning of the 14th week before the expected week of childbirth (i.e. her 26th week of pregnancy) are entitled to additional maternity leave of up to 26 weeks, beginning at the end of the ordinary maternity leave. It is important to work out this date, as not only is it relevant to the entitlement for additional maternity leave, but also it is relevant to statutory maternity pay and to the notification requirements. It is referred to in this chapter as the 'Calculation Date'.

Employees who have taken ordinary maternity leave or additional maternity leave normally have the right to return to the same job.

These rights to ordinary maternity leave and additional maternity leave apply where a woman gives birth to a living child or has a stillbirth after 24 weeks of pregnancy.

Ordinary maternity leave

1. Duration

Maternity leave may not commence before the start of the 11th week before the beginning of the week in which the baby is due. Subject to this, maternity leave begins on the date the employee tells her employer she intends her leave to start. However, maternity leave can begin earlier than the date the employee chooses if she is absent from work for a reason which is wholly or partly because of her pregnancy. The Department of Social Security publishes a free leaflet, *Pregnancy Related Illnesses NI200*, which sets out the illnesses which are recognised as being connected to pregnancy. In these circumstances, her maternity leave shall begin on the first day of her absence, provided that date is after the beginning of the fourth week before the start of the week the baby is due.

Women are prohibited from working within two weeks of childbirth. It is a criminal offence for an employer to fail to comply with this prohibition.

2. Notification

An employee is only entitled to maternity leave if she gives the required notice of:

- the fact that she is pregnant;
- the expected week her baby is due (or the date of the birth in the unlikely event that it has already occurred); and
- the date she wishes her leave to begin.

Notification must be given by the Calculation Date or, if that is not possible, as soon as is reasonably practicable thereafter. If the employer so requests, the employee must produce a certificate from a registered medical practitioner or midwife stating the expected week the baby is due.

If the maternity leave period has started before the notified leave date, either due to pregnancy-related absence or the employee giving birth, the employee must notify her employer as soon as she can that she is absent for whatever reason. If the employer requests, this notification must be in writing.

Once an employer has received notification from an employee as set out above, it must write to the employee within 28 days setting out the date on which the employee's full entitlement to maternity leave will end. For a model letter acknowledging notification of maternity leave, please see Appendix 18.

3. Rights during maternity leave

During maternity leave an employee is entitled to all the benefits that she would have received had she not been on maternity leave, except wages and salary (but including benefits in kind). This means that the contract of employment continues and the period on maternity leave counts towards her continuity of employment.

4. Contractual rights

It is not uncommon for an employee's employment contract to grant more favourable maternity provisions than the statutory rights.

Additional maternity leave

1. Duration

Additional maternity leave may last up to 26 weeks beginning at the end of the ordinary maternity leave period.

2. Notification

No notice needs to be given by the employee of her intentions to take additional maternity leave. It is presumed she will take it unless she notifies otherwise.

3. Rights during additional maternity leave

The contract of employment continues during the additional maternity leave period, but the only terms and conditions that need apply will be the employer's obligations of trust and confidence and the employee's obligations of good faith and any terms and conditions relating to notice of termination, compensation in the event of redundancy, disciplinary or grievance procedures, disclosure of confidential information, the acceptance by the employee of gifts or other benefits or her participation in any other business.

Right to return to work

1. Ordinary maternity leave

An employee returning after 26 weeks' ordinary maternity leave normally has the right to return to the same job that she left. If the job that she left was full-time and she would prefer to work in a more flexible pattern, she may request flexible working (see page 67 for more details). If she wants to return to work before the end of her 26-week leave, she must give her employer at least 28 days' notice of the date she intends to return to work.

2. Additional maternity leave

An employee returning after additional maternity leave has the right to return to the same job that she left or, if that is not reasonably practicable, to another job which is both suitable and appropriate in the circumstances and on terms and conditions which are no less favourable than those which would have applied had she not been absent from work.

If the employer refuses to allow a woman to return from maternity leave, she will be entitled to claim unfair dismissal. Case law would suggest a claim of sex discrimination may also be successful in these circumstances.

Employees are entitled not to be subjected to any detriment by any act or omission of their employer due to the fact that they are pregnant, have given birth to a child, have been suspended from work on maternity grounds, or took or availed themselves of the benefits of ordinary or additional maternity leave.

There is no right for the employee to postpone the return to work after additional maternity leave if she is unfit to return to work. If the employee is sick, the normal company rules on sick leave will apply.

Statutory maternity pay

Statutory maternity pay (SMP) is a payment that employers are required to make to eligible employees, even if the employee does not intend to return to work after the child is born.

Eligibility

An employee only qualifies for SMP if:

- she has stopped work wholly or partly because of pregnancy or childbirth; and

- she has 26 weeks' continuous employment with the same employer by the Calculation Date; and

- her normal weekly earnings in the eight weeks before the start of the 14th week before the expected week of childbirth were above the lower earnings limit for the payment of National Insurance contributions (currently £82) (if the employee's normal weekly earnings are below the lower earnings limit, she can apply for maternity allowance from the DSS on Form SMP1); and

- she has reached the start of the 11th week before the expected week of childbirth (or if she has given birth prior to that date).

Entitlement

The employee is entitled to SMP for 26 weeks (known as the 'maternity pay period') as follows:

- for the first six weeks, 90 per cent of her normal weekly earnings over a reference period of eight weeks immediately before the Calculation Date;

- for the rest of the maternity pay period, a flat rate currently of £106 per week.

SMP is subject to Income Tax, National Insurance contributions and any other regular deductions and should be paid by the same method and at the same time as the employee would normally be paid. If there is no normal agreement as to which day wages are paid on, payment should be made on the last day of the calendar month.

Employers also need to ensure SMP is calculated, or adjusted, to take account of any salary increase received between the start of the reference period and the end of the period when the employee is in receipt of the higher rate of SMP.

The employee may also have a contractual right to maternity pay which the employer may set off against SMP.

How to make a claim for SMP

To make a claim, the employee simply gives her employer 28 days' notification that she will be absent because of her pregnancy or as much notice as is practicable. The employee may change this date but must give 28 days' notice of the new date. The employer is obliged to complete various forms. The government-run Employers' Helpline can provide further details on 0845 714 3143.

The employee is not required to give notice if she leaves the job for a reason wholly unconnected with her pregnancy after the Calculation Date. She must, however, give her employer notice of the date on which she actually went into labour if this fell before the 11th week before the expected week of childbirth.

If requested, the employee must also provide her employer with a maternity certificate completed by a doctor or registered midwife as evidence of her pregnancy and expected week of childbirth.

Remedies for non-payment of SMP

If the employer fails to pay SMP or the employee disputes the amount paid, the employee has the right to require from her employer a written statement of what SMP it considers to be due and the reasons why.

If nothing is resolved, the matter may be referred to an adjudication officer. An appeal regarding the adjudication officer's decision may be made to the Social Security Appeals Tribunal and a further appeal may be put forward, on a point of law only, to the Social Security Commissioners.

Reclaiming SMP

The employer may reclaim at least 92 per cent of the gross amount of SMP it has paid by deducting it from the total (i.e. both primary and secondary)

Class 1 National Insurance contributions due to be paid for all employees in that tax month.

Small employers whose annual gross National Insurance bill does not exceed £45,000 are entitled to recover 100 per cent of SMP paid, plus additional compensation of 4.5 per cent of total SMP paid.

Adoption rights

The statutory rights that apply to employees (male or female) who adopt a child mirror as closely as possible the provisions for maternity rights and are as follows:

- The right to take adoption leave (and return to work)
- Protection from dismissal and detrimental treatment
- Statutory adoption pay

The right to take adoption leave

Any employee who satisfies the following conditions will have the right to take ordinary adoption leave. The employee must:

- have been matched with a child by an adoption agency;
- have at least 26 weeks' continuous service by the week the employee is notified of the match;
- be legally adopting the child;
- have given proper notice to the employer of his intention to take leave;
- have produced to his employer evidence of his entitlement to take adoption leave.

Adoption leave is not available where the child is already known to the adopters, for example, in step-family adoptions or adoptions by existing foster carers.

If a couple are adopting a child jointly, only one partner will be able to take adoption leave. The employee must provide the employer with a document issued by the matching adoption agency stating:

- the name and address of the agency;

- the name and address of the employee;

- the date on which the employee was first notified of the match; and

- the date on which the agency expects to place the child.

All employees who have taken ordinary adoption leave are also entitled to take additional adoption leave for a period of 26 weeks, beginning on the day after the last day of ordinary adoption leave.

Notification

The employee must give notice of his intentions to take ordinary adoption leave within seven days of having been notified of a match, unless this is not reasonably practicable. The notice must specify:

- the expected date of placement;

- the date on which the leave will commence.

If the employer so requests, such notice should be given in writing. Once the employer has received this notification, it must respond to the employee setting out in writing the date the employee's adoption leave will end. Please see Appendix 19 for a model letter of acknowledgement.

Rights during adoption leave

During ordinary adoption leave, the employee is entitled to all the benefits that he would have received had he not been on adoption leave, with the exception of wages and salary (but including benefits in kind). This means that the contract of employment continues and the period of ordinary adoption leave counts towards the employee's continuity of employment.

The contract of employment also continues during the additional adoption leave period, but the only terms and conditions that need apply will be the employer's obligations of trust and confidence and the employee's obligations of good faith and any terms and conditions relating to the notice of termination, compensation in the event of redundancy, disciplinary or grievance procedures, disclosure of confidential information, the acceptance by the employee of gifts or other benefits, or his participation in any other business.

Right to return to work

1. Ordinary adoption leave

An employee returning after 26 weeks' ordinary adoption leave normally has the right to return to the same job that he left. If he wants to return to work before the end of the 26-week period, he must give the employer at least 28 days' notice of the date he intends to return to work.

2. Additional adoption leave

An employee returning after additional adoption leave has the right to return to the same job that he left, or if that is not reasonably practicable, to another job that is both suitable and appropriate in the circumstances and on terms and conditions which are no less favourable than those which would have applied and with the same seniority and pension rights had he not taken adoption leave.

Protection from dismissal and detrimental treatment

Dismissal or selection for redundancy of any employee who took or sought to take adoption leave is automatically unfair, regardless of his length of service or hours of work. However, there is an important exemption for small companies which employ fewer than five employees where it is not reasonably practicable to allow the employee on adoption leave to return to a job which is both suitable and appropriate or, in these circumstances, an associated employer offers the employee a suitable and appropriate job, yet the employee unreasonably refuses it. In these specific circumstances, the dismissal would not be automatically unfair. There is no similar exemption in maternity legislation.

Statutory adoption pay

Statutory adoption pay (SAP) is a payment that employers are required to make to eligible employees, even if the employee does not intend to return to work after taking adoption leave.

Eligibility

An employee only qualifies for SAP if:

- he has stopped work because of adoption leave;
- he has 26 weeks' continuous employment with the same employer by the date he has been notified of the match;
- he is a person with whom a child is, or is expected to be, placed for adoption;
- he has normal weekly earnings of above the lower earnings limit for the payment of National Insurance contributions (currently £82);
- he has not elected to receive statutory paternity pay.

Entitlement

The employee is entitled to SAP for 26 weeks at the current standard rate of £106 per week (or 90 per cent of average weekly earnings if this is less than £106 per week).

SAP is subject to Income Tax, National Insurance contributions and any other regular deductions and should be paid by the same method and at the same time as the employee would normally be paid. If there is no normal agreement as to which day wages are paid, payment should be made on the last day of the calendar month.

The employee may also have a contractual right to adoption pay which the employer may offset against SAP.

How to make a claim for SAP

To make a claim, the employee simply gives his employer 28 days' notification of the date from which he expects SAP will be paid, unless this is not reasonably practicable.

Where an employee who is entitled to receive SAP leaves his employment before the adoption pay period has begun, he will still be eligible to receive SAP. SAP payments will commence on the date of the child's placement or, if the termination of employment occurs on or within 14 days before the expected date of placement, on the day immediately following the last day of his employment.

Reclaiming SAP

The rules for reclaiming SAP are the same as the rules for reclaiming SMP.

Parental leave

Employees have a right to take 13 weeks' unpaid leave for the purpose of caring for a child, subject to satisfying certain qualified conditions. Parents of disabled children have a right to take 18 weeks' unpaid leave.

What is parental leave?

Parental leave may be taken not just in connection with caring for a child's health. For example, it can be used for the purposes of settling the child into a playgroup, taking a child on holiday or simply staying at home with the child.

Qualifying conditions

A person qualifies for the right to parental leave if he is an employee with at least one year's continuous service and has, or expects to have, responsibility for a child. A person has responsibility for a child in the following circumstances:

- He or she is the natural mother or father, who were married at the time of birth.

- She is the natural mother where the parents were not married at the time of birth.

- He is the natural father where the parents were not married at the time of birth if the father acquires parental responsibility by court order or by agreement with the mother.

- He or she is a legal guardian.

- He or she is an adoptive parent.

The relevant child must have been under five on 15 December 1999 or if the child is an adopted child, the child must have been adopted after 15 December 1994.

It is a fundamental principle that the right to parental leave is an individual one and will be non-transferable. This means that both parents will be able to take up to 13 weeks' leave if they are both working, but they will not be able to add their leave entitlement so that one employee can take more than 13 weeks and the other less. This is clearly designed to encourage fathers to take parental leave. If a man does not use his leave, it will simply go to waste.

When can parental leave be taken?

Parental leave may be taken before the child's fifth birthday or where he has been adopted, during a period of five years or up to the age of 18, whichever is the sooner. An exception to this is where the employer has postponed parental leave; in such circumstances it would be possible to have the postponed leave taken after the fifth birthday or anniversary of the adoption cut-off point. Also, where a child is entitled to a disability living allowance, parental leave may be taken at any time up to the child's 18th birthday. Parental leave may not be taken in periods of less than a week and any fraction of a week will be treated as a whole week. The exception to this is in cases where the child is entitled to a disability living allowance.

Rights during parental leave

The employment relationship continues during the leave period, although leave may be unpaid. The employment relationship continues in exactly the same way as in the case of a person taking maternity leave, namely, the employee is entitled to the benefit of his employer's implied obligation to him of trust and confidence and is also bound by his implied obligation of good faith and any expressed obligation prohibiting disclosure of confidential information or the employee's participation in any competing business.

Right to return to work

An employee taking parental leave for a period of more than four weeks or immediately after additional maternity leave has the right to return to his old job at the end of the leave period. Alternatively, if it is not reasonably practicable for him to return to his old job, he has the right to return to another job which is both suitable for the individual and appropriate in the circumstances. The terms and conditions on which the individual may return to work after parental leave are as follows:

- as to remuneration, no less favourable than those which would have been applicable to him had he not been absent from work;

- with seniority, pension rights and similar rights as they would have been if the period prior to his parental leave were continuous with his employment following his return to work; and

- no less favourable than those which have been applicable to him had he not been absent from work during the period of parental leave.

Parental leave schemes

The government has indicated that it would like employers to agree their own parental leave schemes that suit the needs of its business and employees. However, in order to implement a legally enforceable parental scheme, it is necessary for this to be entered into by way of a collective agreement or a workforce agreement. A collective agreement is one which is reached between the union and an employer as a result of collective bargaining. A workforce agreement is, in effect, a sort of collective agreement which does not involve a union as such. It is an agreement between an employer and its workers which satisfies certain conditions. The agreement has to be in writing and cannot be in effect for more than five years. It has to apply to all members of the workforce or all members of the workforce who belong to a particular group. It has to be signed either by representatives of the workforce or group or, where there are 20 or fewer employees, by appropriate representatives or the majority of the employees. This is a fairly complex procedure and it is therefore recommended that if the employer wishes to implement its own parental leave scheme by means of a workforce agreement, further advice should be sought.

If the employer does not implement its own parental leave scheme, the legislation provides that default provisions automatically come into play. These provide that an employee can only exercise his entitlement to parental leave if:

- he has complied with a reasonable request made by the employer to produce evidence of entitlement to take parental leave and the child's date of birth or the date on which a placement began for an adopted child;

- he has given his employer proper notice; and

- the employer does not postpone the leave period.

The amount of notice which the employee must give the employer before taking parental leave is 21 days. When leave is to begin either on the birth of a child or on the placement of a child for adoption, the notice must be given at least 21 days before the beginning of the expected week of childbirth or week of placement. The default provisions also provide that an employee may not take more than four weeks' leave in respect of any individual child during a 12-month period.

Postponement of parental leave

The employer can postpone when a period of parental leave may be taken, except where it is to be taken on the birth or placement of a child. In every other circumstance, the employer can postpone parental leave if the employer considers that the operation of the business would be unduly disrupted. The employer must agree to allow the employee to take the same period of leave within six months at least. To postpone, the employer must give notice within seven days after the employee's notice requesting leave was given to the employer.

Enforcement

An employee has a right to make a claim in the employment tribunal if his employer unreasonably postpones, or refuses, or attempts to prevent, the grant of parental leave. Compensation is such as the tribunal considers just and equitable, taking into account the employer's behaviour and the loss sustained by the employee as a result of the matter complained of.

Employees also have protection from being subjected to any detriment by any act or omission by the employer because they took or sought to take parental leave. The employee also has protection from automatic unfair dismissal if he is dismissed for a reason relating to the fact that he took parental leave.

There is no statutory requirement for an employer to keep records of when parental leave has been taken. In practice, it is highly likely that organisations will need to keep some sort of record. When an employee changes employer, he will need to requalify for parental leave and has no right to take more than 13 weeks for each child in total, including any leave that may have been taken with the previous employer. Therefore, when an employer requests a reference from a previous employer, it would be sensible to ask it to provide details of whether parental leave has been taken by the individual and, if so, how much.

Time off for dependants

All employees (regardless of service) are entitled to take a reasonable amount of unpaid leave to deal with incidents involving a dependant.

Dependants are defined as the employee's parent, wife, husband or partner, child or someone who lives as part of the family. The employee has the right to time off:

- to help when a dependant is ill or injured;
- to cope when the arrangements for caring for a dependant unexpectedly break down;
- when a dependant gives birth;
- when a dependant dies; or
- to deal with an unexpected incident involving a dependant child during school hours or on a school trip.

In the first two cases, the dependant could also be someone who relies on the employee in a particular emergency.

No predetermined maximum is set on the amount of time off which can be taken. However, it is envisaged by the government that one or two days will usually be the most that are needed to deal with the immediate issues and to sort out longer-term arrangements if necessary.

An employee may complain to an employment tribunal if his employer unreasonably refuses to permit him to take time off for dependants. If the tribunal finds the complaint well-founded, compensation may be awarded that the tribunal considers just and equitable in all the circumstances, having regard to the employer's default and any loss sustained by the employee which is attributable to the matters complained of.

Employees also have protection from detriment by any act or omission by the employer because they took or sought to take time off for dependants.

Paternity rights

Paternity leave

Many people think that paternity leave is only available for men. However, in the case of same-sex partners, paternity leave may be available to a female employee who has an enduring relationship with the child's mother. Any employee who satisfies the following conditions as to an expected child will have the right to take paternity leave. The employee must:

- have at least 26 weeks' continuous service by the beginning of the 14th week before the expected week for childbirth or in the case of an adopted child, by the beginning of the week the adopter is notified of being matched with the child;

- have a relationship with the child;

- be the biological father of the child or be married to or have an enduring relationship with the child's mother.

Notification

An employee wishing to take paternity leave must give the required notice of:

- the expected week of the birth of the child, or if the birth has already occurred, the actual date of the child's birth, or the date of placement if the child is adopted;

- the period of leave to be taken (which may be in one block of either one or two weeks); and

- the date on which the leave will commence.

Paternity leave must be taken within 56 days of the expected week of childbirth or placement. Eligible employees can choose to take either one week or two consecutive weeks' paternity leave (not odd days).

Rights during paternity leave

During paternity leave, the employee is entitled to all benefits that he would have received had he not been on paternity leave, except wages and salary (but including benefits in kind). This means that the contract of employment continues and the period on paternity leave counts towards the employee's continuity of employment.

Statutory paternity pay

Statutory paternity pay (SPP) is a payment that employers are required to make to eligible employees, even if the employees do not intend to work after the child is born.

Eligibility and entitlement

An employee shall qualify for SPP (which is currently at the rate of £106 per week) if:

- he has a right to take paternity leave;
- he has normal weekly earnings that are above the lower earnings limit for the payment of National Insurance contributions (currently £82);
- he gives at least 28 days' notice (unless this is not reasonably practicable) of the date from which he expects SPP to be paid; and
- he has completed a self-declaration that he is entitled to receive SPP.

Reclaiming SPP

The rules for reclaiming SPP are the same rules as for reclaiming SMP.

Right to return to work after paternity leave

An employee returning after paternity leave has the right to return to the same job. The employee also has the right not to be subjected to any detrimental dismissal because he took or sought to take paternity leave and any such dismissal will be automatically unfair. Please note that the same exemption for small companies applies in relation to adoption leave.

Flexible working

Certain employees (male or female) have the statutory right to make a request to adopt flexible working arrangements to care for a child.

Eligibility

To be eligible for such a request the employee must:

- have a child under six or if a child is disabled, under 18 years of age; and

- have been continuously employed for at least 26 weeks at the date of making the request;

- be making the request to enable him to care for the child;

- have responsibility or expect to have responsibility for the child;

- be a biological parent, guardian, adopter or foster carer of the child; or

- be married to or be the partner of and/or live with the biological parent, guardian, adopter or foster carer of the child; and

- not have made another application to work flexibly in the past 12 months.

Making an application

Employees making an application to work flexibly must do so in writing, stating:

- that the application is being made under the statutory right to request a flexible working pattern; and

- that he has responsibility for the upbringing of the child and he is either the mother, father, adopter, guardian or foster parent, or is married to, or is the partner of, the child's mother, father, adopter, guardian or foster parent;

- the flexible working pattern he is applying for and the date he would like it to become effective;

- what effect, if any, he thinks the proposed change will have on the employer and how, in his opinion, any such effect may be dealt with; and

- whether a previous application has been made to the employer and, if so, when it was made.

Considering the application

The employer has a legal obligation to consider any request to work flexibly and within 28 days it must hold a meeting with the employee to discuss the application and any possible compromises. The employee may be accompanied at this meeting by a fellow worker, a full-time trade union official or a lay union official who has been suitably trained. The employer must notify the employee of its decision within a further 14 days.

If the employer accepts the application, then the parties will need to discuss what arrangements will need to be made for when the working pattern is changed.

Right to refuse request to work flexibly

An employer may refuse the request only when there is a clear business reason. The business grounds for refusing an application must be from one of those below:

- Burden of additional costs.

- Detrimental effect on ability to meet customer demand.

- Inability to reorganise work among existing staff.

- Inability to recruit additional staff.

- Detrimental impact on quality.

- Detrimental impact on performance.

- Insufficiency of work during the work period proposed.

- Planned structural changes.

If the employer does refuse the request, it is essential that it gives a full explanation of the reasons why it is doing so.

Appeal

An employee has 14 days to appeal in writing after the date of notification of the employer's decision. If an appeal is made, the employer must arrange an appeal meeting to take place within 14 days of the appeal. The employee may be accompanied at the appeal meeting by a fellow worker, full-time trade union official or lay union official who has been suitably trained. Following the appeal meeting, the employee must be informed of the outcome of the appeal in writing within 14 days.

Remedies

An employee can present a complaint to an employment tribunal on the grounds that the employer has:

- failed to comply with its statutory duties in relation to the employee's application to work flexibly; or

- based its decision to reject the application on incorrect facts.

The employee must first exhaust the employer's appeal process. The employee must make the complaint within three months of either the date on which the employee was notified of the appeal decision or the date on which the alleged breach of the employer's duty was committed.

The tribunal does not have the power to order an employer to implement a flexible working arrangement. However, claims under discrimination legislation can still be brought. Therefore, a female employee returning from maternity leave and being refused the right to work part-time, for example, may still have a valid claim for indirect sex discrimination.

CHAPTER 4

Sickness benefit

Subject to satisfying certain conditions, all employees are entitled to receive statutory sick pay (SSP) from their employers when they are absent from work for four or more consecutive days up to a limit of 28 weeks. Unless the employee has a contractual right to normal pay, SSP is all the employer is obliged to pay him during sickness. The model contract included in this book (see Appendix 11) provides for normal remuneration for a limited period. The current weekly rate of SSP is £68.20 and this rate is verifiable by looking at the Department for Work and Pensions' website (www.dwp.gov.uk) or by contacting ACAS (see Appendix 32 for their contact details). Also, for full instructions about SSP see the Inland Revenue's *Statutory Sick Pay Manual for Employers CA30* and for specific enquiries contact their Employers' Helpline on 0845 714 3143.

Eligibility

Employees are not eligible for SSP if on the first day of the period of incapacity for work (or PIW – see overleaf):

- they are aged under 16 or over 65;

- they have a contract of services which is for a specified period of three months or less (and it has not been extended);

- their average weekly pay is below the point at which National Insurance contributions are payable (currently £82);

- they have received social security benefit in the 57 days before the first day of sickness;

- they have not yet commenced working;

- they become sick while pregnant during the statutory maternity pay period (see chapter 3);

- they have been due SSP for 28 weeks from a former employer and the last day on which SSP was paid is eight weeks ago or less;

- they become sick during a trade dispute at their workplace, unless they can prove they have no direct interest in the dispute;

- they are in legal custody.

If an employer is notified that an ineligible employee has been absent for four or more consecutive days, it must send a form to the employee within seven days of being notified which explains why SSP is not payable. The employee may then claim incapacity benefit.

Requirements for qualification

SSP is only payable:

- if the employee has been incapable of work for four or more consecutive days (this is known as a period of incapacity for work or 'PIW');

- if the employee has notified the employer of his absence and given evidence of his incapacity, i.e. a doctor's note (in accordance with any rules laid down by the employer which must be made available to all employees);

- for days on which the employee would normally be required to work;

- during a 'period of entitlement', i.e. a period commencing with the start of PIW and ending:

  1. when the employee returns to work;

2. when the maximum entitlement of 28 weeks' SSP has been paid (if the employee is still sick in these circumstances, he shall become entitled to incapacity benefit);

3. with the expiry or termination of the employee's contract of employment;

4. when the employee becomes entitled to maternity allowance or statutory maternity pay (see chapter 3); or

5. if the employee goes into legal custody.

If the employer does not make its own rules regarding notification of sickness, the law states that an employee must tell the company of any date he is unfit for work no later than seven calendar days after that day. If the employee does not notify the employer of his sickness absence within the stated time limit and the employer considers there was a good cause for delay, it must accept that the employee notified the employer correctly if it is given within one calendar month of the date stated by the employer or of the seven-day period after the relevant day of incapacity (this may be extended to 91 days if it is not reasonably practicable to notify the employer within one month).

If there are less than eight weeks between any periods of incapacity for work, they are linked and count as one PIW for SSP purposes.

When calculating whether the maximum entitlement has been paid, periods of entitlement to SSP from a previous employer are taken into account:

- where less than eight weeks have elapsed between the last day the previous employer was liable to pay the employee SSP and the start of the PIW with the new employer; and

- the employee has provided the new employer with a leaver's statement (Form SSP1(L)) or the employer has issued such a statement to the employee.

Employers must issue a Form SSP(I)(T) to employees whose maximum entitlement to 28 weeks is about to expire, no later than the 23rd week of sickness.

SSP attracts Income Tax and National Insurance contributions.

Employers cannot require employees to contract out of their rights to SSP or contribute towards SSP payments. Failure to comply with the obligation to pay SSP can amount to a criminal offence.

Employers' right to reimbursement of statutory sickness payments

All employers may reclaim the amount paid out as SSP to the extent that their SSP liability exceeds 13 per cent of their liability to pay National Insurance contributions (both employees' and employers') for the month in question.

Records

All employers must keep records of the dates on which their employees are absent due to sickness for three years. The penalty for failure to meet these obligations is a fine of up to £1,000 plus £40 per day for as long as the offence continues. Employers who produce false information concerning SSP face a fine of up to £5,000 or a maximum of three months in prison.

Employers have the freedom from operating the SSP scheme if they pay sick employees contractual remuneration at or above the prescribed rate of SSP.

CHAPTER 5
Discrimination

The law on discrimination has an enormous effect in employment. The UK's membership in the European Union (EU) means that a high level of protection from discrimination exists for employees. An employee who complains of discrimination in whatever way can pursue legal action in an employment tribunal and no qualifying period is necessary in order to bring such a claim. Discrimination claims are not subject to any maximum award and are therefore increasing in number and value.

UK legislation that governs discrimination complies with the EU law; when new EU laws are introduced, UK laws must be amended accordingly. There is currently protection from discrimination in relation to sex, gender reassignment (i.e. 'sex change'), marital status, race, disability, trade union membership, sexual orientation and religion or religious belief.

The areas of discrimination that are considered in this chapter are:

- Sex, marriage or gender reassignment
- Race
- Disability
- Sexual orientation
- Religion or belief

Harassment on the grounds of all of the above is also a recognised form of discrimination and is considered separately in this chapter. Unequal treatment on the ground of sex is also protected by the law on equal pay and this is also considered in this chapter.

Sex discrimination and discrimination on the ground of marriage

Discrimination on the grounds of sex or marriage is made unlawful by the Sex Discrimination Act 1975 (SDA), which forbids it at every stage of employment (i.e. advertising vacancies, engagement of employees, promotion, training and other opportunities, and dismissal). Employment has a wider definition in the SDA than other employment protection legislation, protecting not only individuals who are employees but also individuals working under a contract for services and partners in a partnership. In addition, other organisations, including trade unions, trade or professional associations and employment agencies, must also observe the provisions of the SDA.

Individuals who are not protected by the SDA in their employment are:

- persons who work wholly or mainly outside Great Britain;
- police officers in relation to height requirements and uniform or uniform allowances;
- prison officers in relation to height requirements;
- ministers of religion if employment is limited to one sex in order to comply with the doctrines of the religion or to avoid offending the religious sensibilities of a significant number of its followers.

Definition of discrimination

There are four recognised forms of discrimination:

1. Direct discrimination
2. Indirect discrimination
3. Victimisation
4. Harassment

In deciding whether discrimination has occurred, the position of the person allegedly discriminated against is compared to that of a person of similar skill and qualification. The intention or motive of the alleged discriminator is irrelevant. The SDA protects males as well as females.

1. Direct discrimination

Direct discrimination is easy to recognise: it occurs where an employee has received less favourable treatment and would not have but for his sex or marital status. For there to be direct discrimination, the person's sex or marital status is the basis of the particular decision which results in the individual being deprived in some way and which gives rise to less favourable treatment. It is the treatment itself rather than its consequences which must be different and less favourable.

An individual may exercise unconscious prejudices because of his upbringing and perceptions, without being aware of the fact and this can amount to direct discrimination. It is important that employers give training in order to avoid such prejudices.

In order to succeed in an employment tribunal with a complaint of discrimination, the individual complaining of discrimination would only need to bring evidence that would lead the tribunal to presume or infer that there has been discrimination. It would then be up to the employer to disprove this presumption or inference. If the employer could not disprove it and there was a finding of direct discrimination, no question of justification for the employer's treatment could arise.

Dress requirements. The test of whether or not the individual would have received the same treatment but for his sex has proved problematic where the treatment complained of is the imposition of dress requirements. Therefore, there is no discrimination where male and female employees are subject to different but comparable dress requirements.

Maternity cases. Unfavourable treatment on the grounds of an employee's pregnancy or for other maternity-related reasons is direct discrimination contrary to the SDA. There is no need for a comparison with a male employee: once a female employee has established that her treatment amounted to direct discrimination, no question of justification for this treatment can arise.

This occurs when a woman is engaged by the employer for an indefinite period. However, if a woman is employed for a single fixed-term period or to fulfil a particular task, it is uncertain whether the employer would be guilty of discrimination if the woman was denied employment during which time she would be unavailable for work because of her pregnancy or, if after engaging the woman for such a period, the employer discovered that she was pregnant and subsequently cancelled the agreement.

2. Indirect discrimination

Indirect discrimination covers other forms of less obvious discriminatory treatment. Indirect discrimination takes place where:

- an employer imposes a condition or practice which is to the individual's detriment;

- the condition or practice can be shown to have a disproportionate impact in excluding others of the individual's sex or marital status; and

- the condition or practice cannot be justified, irrespective of the individual's sex or marital status.

Please note that there is no requirement for the individual to show that he cannot comply with the condition or practice; he just needs to show it is to his detriment.

For example, indirect sex discrimination would take place where an employer imposed a requirement for all employees to be subject to a five-foot maximum height requirement. A much larger proportion of women than men would be able to meet this requirement and the employer would have to justify the reason for imposing such a condition. If the reason was because the job was to crew a boat with very low ceilings, such a requirement would probably be justified. But if the reason was because the employer wished to provide only one size of uniform, the employer would be indirectly discriminating against men.

Justification requires an objective balance between the discriminatory effect of the condition or practice and the reasonable needs of the employer who is applying it. Justification is a 'matter of fact' for the employment tribunal, which means that one tribunal might reach one conclusion and another might reach a different conclusion.

Age. Although there is no law against age discrimination, placing restrictions on age can, in some circumstances, amount to indirect sex discrimination. This has been the case where an employer required a maximum age limit of 28 for a job. An employment appeal tribunal held this was indirectly discriminatory because in practice it was harder for women to comply with it than men, since women in their 20s are commonly fully occupied with childbearing.

3. Victimisation

An employer would be guilty of sex discrimination by victimisation if it treated any employee less favourably than others because that employee had brought or threatened to bring proceedings, give evidence or information, or take any action or make any allegation concerning the employer, with reference to the SDA or the Equal Pay Act 1970 (EPA).

4. Harassment

See page 97.

Exceptions to sex discrimination protection

The law recognises that there are some circumstances where there may be a good reason to give favourable treatment to a particular sex. In particular, there are two areas:

- **Positive discrimination.** If an employer identifies that one sex is not properly represented within certain work areas, it may try to encourage individuals of that particular sex to apply, by providing training or through an advertising campaign. Before doing this, the employer must be able to show that in the previous 12 months there has been either no individuals of that particular sex or only a small proportion of them carrying out the work in question. If not, the positive action will be discriminatory.

- **Genuine occupational qualifications.** For some jobs being of a certain sex is a requirement, as set out in chapter 1. But attitudes and cultures are changing and an exception which was once acceptable may no longer be so. The applicability of the genuine occupational qualification exception should be considered every time a vacancy is advertised.

Employer responsibility for discrimination

Under the SDA an employer is liable for anything done by its employees in the course of their employment, whether or not it was done with the employer's knowledge or approval. This ensures that the employer takes responsibility for preventing discrimination at work (in the SDA 'employment' has a wide definition and includes any contract personally to execute work and is not confined to a contract of service). However, it is a defence if the employer can prove that it took such steps as were practicable to prevent an employee from doing a certain act.

If the employer wishes to rely on this defence, it must be shown that positive steps have been taken to address the possibility of discrimination occurring in the workplace. For example, the employer should introduce and adhere to an equal opportunities policy which incorporates a sexual and racial harassment policy (see Appendix 14). All employees should be aware of such policies and be given training in their obligations not to discriminate. Disciplinary action should be taken against those who do discriminate.

The individual discriminator still risks that action will be taken against him whether or not the employer is found responsible. An individual who wishes to pursue an action for discrimination may issue proceedings in an employment tribunal against his employer and against the individual discriminator. However, if the individual discriminator can prove that the action taken was based on an assurance from the employer that it was not discriminatory, he will not be held liable for discrimination.

Other unlawful acts under the SDA

It is unlawful to:

- aid and abet someone knowingly in unlawful discrimination; the person who committed the discriminatory act has the defence that he acted reasonably, relying on a statement by the other that the act would not be unlawful;

- instruct someone to discriminate over whom one has authority or to someone who normally acts in accordance with one's wishes;

- induce or attempt to induce someone to discriminate; such inducements may include offering either benefits or detriments.

No contracting-out

Employers are not allowed to exclude or limit any provision of the SDA in a contract of employment. If they do, it would have no effect, leaving the employee at liberty to bring a complaint under the SDA against the employer in an employment tribunal.

Equal Opportunities Commission (EOC)

The SDA established the EOC, which has the duty to:

- work towards the elimination of discrimination;

- promote equality of opportunity between men and women generally; and

- keep under review the work of the SDA and the EPA (for more details on the EPA, see page 100).

Codes of practice. The EOC has issued a code of practice and guidance notes for the elimination of sex and marriage discrimination and the promotion of equality of opportunity in employment. Employers are advised to review the code and guidance notes and to put into place its recommendations. A breach of the recommendations does not of itself render a person liable to proceedings, but it may be taken into account by an employment tribunal when determining whether or not discrimination has occurred.

Investigations. As part of its general duties the EOC may, if it thinks fit and if required by the Secretary of State for Education and Employment, conduct a formal investigation (which may be in relation to a particular organisation) where it considers there has been a breach of the provisions of the SDA or the EPA.

Non-discrimination notice. The EOC can issue a non-discrimination notice if it finds that a person has committed or is committing an unlawful discriminatory act or practice, a breach of the provisions relating to advertising or a term modified (or included) by virtue of an equality clause, or has given instructions to discriminate or pressured to discriminate. This notice may require a person to stop committing any such acts or to change any of his practices or arrangements, to inform the EOC that he has effected those changes and what they are, and to take such steps to inform people affected by those practices or arrangements. The EOC cannot issue a non-discrimination notice without:

1. informing the relevant person of its intention and the grounds of the notice;

2. allowing the relevant person at least 28 days in which to make representations; and

3. taking into account all the representations made by him.

Employers are advised to ensure that they do not breach any of the provisions of the SDA or the EPA. If they do, and are informed of a proposal to issue a notice, they must take action to prevent the discrimination. If a notice has been issued and employers do not wish to challenge it, they should comply with it as soon as possible. An employer has a right of appeal against any requirement of a non-discrimination notice.

A register of non-discrimination notices which have been issued is available for inspection and for copying from the EOC (see Appendix 32 for their contact details).

Gender reassignment

The SDA also prohibits direct discrimination on the ground that a person intends to undergo, is undergoing, or has undergone, a sex change. There is no protection against indirect discrimination.

As with claims of sex discrimination, an allegation of gender reassignment discrimination will not succeed if the defendant can show that a genuine occupational qualification applies, so as to justify the discrimination. The genuine occupational qualifications are those set out in chapter 1, with some further supplementary genuine occupational qualifications created specifically to cover gender reassignment discrimination.

Race discrimination

Discrimination on racial grounds is made unlawful by the Race Relations Act 1976 (RRA), which reflects many of the principles and rules contained in the SDA examined in the first section of this chapter. The RRA forbids less favourable treatment of individuals on racial grounds at every stage of employment. Like the SDA, the RRA protects not only individual employees but also individuals working under a contract for services and partners in a partnership (where the partnership consists of six or more partners). In addition, trade unions, trade or professional associations, employment agencies and other organisations must also observe the provisions of the RRA.

Individuals not protected by the RRA are:

- those who work wholly or mainly outside Great Britain;

- individuals employed by a private household (with the exception of discrimination by victimisation, see page 85).

Definition of discrimination

The four forms of discrimination in relation to sex and on the ground of marriage apply equally to race. Whereas the definitions of sex and marriage are straightforward, what is meant by racial grounds requires further explanation. If a decision is based on an individual's colour, race, nationality or national origins, or ethnic origins, it is a decision based on racial grounds and could be discriminatory.

The meaning of 'ethnic origins' needs clarifying. It has been held that a group has an ethnic origin if it has certain characteristics of:

- a long shared history; and
- a cultural tradition.

Additional relevant characteristics are:

- a common geographical origin or descent from a small number of common ancestors;
- a common language not necessarily peculiar to the group;
- a common literature peculiar to the group;
- a common religion different from that of the neighbouring or surrounding community;
- being a minority or being in an oppressed or dominant group in a large community.

It has been held in the courts that Sikhs are an ethnic group, as are Jews and Gypsies, but at present Rastafarians have been held not to fall within what can be considered an ethnic group.

In a sex discrimination claim, a comparison is made between a female employee and a male employee in equivalent circumstances to decide whether the treatment of one is less favourable. In a race discrimination claim, the comparison must be between the person of the racial or ethnic group and a job applicant or employee who is not of that ethnic or racial group, but whose circumstances are the same, similar or not materially different.

The burden of proof in race discrimination claims differs slightly to the burden of proof in sex discrimination claims. The individual complaining of race discrimination must establish the case and then the employer has to justify the alleged discriminatory act. If no explanation is forthcoming or an unsatisfactory explanation is provided, then the employment tribunal is entitled to infer that discrimination did, in fact, take place.

1. Direct discrimination

The principle of direct discrimination, as already examined in relation to sex and marriage discrimination, applies here: in a race discrimination claim the less favourable treatment is obviously on racial grounds and the test is whether, but for the individual's racial origin, ethnic origin, nationality, national origin or colour, he would not have been subject to that treatment.

2. Indirect discrimination

Broadly, the principle of indirect discrimination as examined in relation to sex and marriage discrimination applies to race discrimination. However, there are some differences. Indirect discrimination will occur if a condition or requirement is imposed which has a disproportionate impact on a particular racial group so that a considerably smaller proportion of members of that group can comply than those outside it, and it cannot be objectively justified on some basis other than colour, race, nationality or ethnic or national origins.

It is necessary for the individual to show that he cannot comply with the condition or requirement and that it is to his detriment. Whether someone can comply with a condition or requirement is decided by what he can do in practice rather than in theory.

The question of whether indirect discrimination is objectively justifiable is (as with sex and marriage discrimination) one of fact for an employment tribunal. The employment tribunal must strike a balance between the discriminatory effect of the condition or requirement being imposed and the reasonable needs of the employer applying it.

3. Victimisation

An employer would be guilty of race discrimination by victimisation if it treated any employee less favourably than others because that employee has already or threatens to bring proceedings, give evidence or information, take any action or make any allegation concerning the employer with reference to the RRA.

4. Harassment

See page 97.

Exceptions to race discrimination protection

As with sex discrimination, the law recognises that in some circumstances there may be a good reason to give favourable treatment to a particular race. There are two areas where exceptions to the law against race discrimination exist:

- **Positive discrimination.** If an employer identifies a particular racial group as not being properly represented within certain work areas, it may try to encourage individuals of that group to apply by providing training or through an advertising campaign. The employer must be able to show that in the previous 12 months there have been either no individuals of the racial group or only a small proportion of them carrying out the particular work in question. If this exception does not apply, then the positive action will be discriminatory. A booklet entitled *What is Positive Action?* published by the Race Relations Employment Advisory Service (see Appendix 32 for their contact details) provides further explanation of positive race discrimination.

- **Genuine occupational qualifications.** For some jobs belonging to a certain racial group is a requirement, as set out in chapter 1. The number of jobs where a person's race is a genuine occupational qualification is not as high as that concerning a person's sex. The warning that attitudes and cultures are changing should also be remembered in relation to race. The applicability of the genuine occupational qualification exception should be considered every time a vacancy is advertised.

Employer responsibility for discrimination

The same principle applies under the RRA as previously described in relation to the SDA in the first section of this chapter. For an employer relying on this defence, regard will be given to whether a written policy on race discrimination has been issued to employees, whether training has been given and whether disciplinary action has been taken against those guilty of race discrimination.

Other unlawful acts under the RRA

The unlawful acts listed on page 81 in relation to the SDA equally apply to the RRA.

No contracting-out

The ban on contractual clauses excluding or limiting provisions of the SDA equally applies to excluding or limiting those of the RRA.

Commission for Racial Equality (CRE)

The RRA established the CRE, which has the duty to:

- work towards the elimination of discrimination;
- promote equality of opportunity between persons of different racial groups;
- keep under review the working of the RRA.

These duties are the same as the duties of the EOC in relation to sex discrimination and the points previously made about codes of practice, investigations and non-discrimination notices apply equally to the CRE. The address of the CRE is listed in Appendix 32.

Disability discrimination

The Disability Discrimination Act 1995 (DDA) applies to the whole of the UK. It protects people with disabilities against discrimination in all aspects of employment. Breach of the DDA can result in a complaint to an employment tribunal, regardless of the length of service and with no limit to the amount of compensation. The government has produced information booklets on different sections of the DDA; these and the code of practice are available by calling the Disability Rights Commission's Helpline on 0845 762 2633.

The main consequence of the DDA in relation to employment is that it is now unlawful for an employer to discriminate against a disabled person – or someone who has been disabled in the past – in recruitment, terms and conditions of employment, promotion, training (or other benefits), dismissal or by subjecting him to any disadvantage. It is important that the term 'employees' be widely interpreted to include the self-employed and those engaged under a contract of service or apprenticeship (as it is with other discrimination legislation).

Code of practice

This gives practical guidance to employers on fulfilling their obligations and avoiding possible claims of discrimination. Breaches of the code are admissible as evidence in employment tribunal hearings.

What kind of discrimination is covered by the DDA?

A disability is defined in this context as a physical or mental impairment which has a substantial and long-term adverse effect on a person's ability to carry out normal day-to-day activities. Such a broad definition includes learning disabilities, mental illnesses (if recognised by a respected body of medical opinion), impairments which come and go if the actual effect is likely to recur (e.g. rheumatoid arthritis) and severe disfigurements. People with progressive conditions are covered from the moment the condition leads to impairment of their ability to carry out day-to-day activities. To be long term, the condition must not be of a temporary nature and must have lasted 12 months or more, or be likely to last 12 months or more. The definition specifically excludes some impairments, such as alcohol or drug addiction, hayfever and self-disfigurement (i.e. tattoos).

Stress, which affects so many people nowadays in many different ways, will not, on its own, amount to a disability. However, if the stress is or becomes sufficiently serious to be a clinically recognised stress-related illness, this may amount to a disability within the Disability Discrimination Act.

To access whether a condition is a disability in this context the best guidance is in a document issued by the government entitled *Guidance on Matters to be Taken in Account in Determining Questions Relating to the Definition of Disability*. A copy can be obtained by calling 0845 762 2633. The Disability Rights Commission may also be able to assist you.

What is discrimination in this context?

An employer discriminates against a disabled person if:

- it treats him less favourably, on the ground of the person's disability. This is known as direct discrimination and can never be justified; or

- it treats him less favourably, for a reason related to the person's present or past disability, than it treats or would treat a person to whom that reason does not apply, and the employer cannot show that this treatment is justified; or

- it fails to comply with a duty of making reasonable adjustments in relation to disabled persons.

As with other forms of discrimination, there is also protection against harassment on the grounds of disability and victimisation.

Justification

Note that justification can only be used as a defence where discrimination occurs in the second of the three forms of discrimination above. Less favourable treatment of a disabled person is justified (and therefore not unlawful) if the reason for it is both 'material' to the circumstances of the case and 'substantial'. This means that the reason has to relate to the individual circumstances in question and must not be trivial or minor.

Reasonable adjustments

If any physical feature of the employer's premises or other arrangements cause a substantial disadvantage to a disabled person, the employer must make reasonable adjustments to prevent it. The term 'arrangements' includes everything that an employer arranges in the workplace and when it co-ordinates the recruitment of employees, for example, selection and interview procedures and working conditions.

Appropriate adjustments may include altering premises, reallocating duties, transferring staff to fill an existing vacancy, altering working hours, assigning someone to a different place of work, allowing absences from office training, acquiring or modifying equipment, modifying instructions or manuals, modifying procedures for testing or assessment and providing a reader or supervision. Whether it is reasonable for an employer to have to make a particular adjustment will depend upon a number of factors:

- How effective it would be in preventing the disadvantage.

- How practical it is.

- The financial and other costs involved and the disruption likely to be caused.

- The extent of the financial resources of the employer.

- The availability of assistance to make the adjustment.

Disability Rights Commission

This advises the government on relevant issues, including the operation of legislation, although it does not have as many powers as the Equal Opportunities Commission or the Commission for Racial Equality in investigating or supporting individuals' complaints.

Sexual orientation discrimination

Discrimination on the ground of sexual orientation is made unlawful by the Employment Equality (Sexual Orientation) Regulations 2003, which forbids such discrimination at every stage of employment (i.e. in advertising vacancies, engagement of employees, promotion, training and other opportunities, and dismissal). Protection is given not only to individuals who are employees but also to a wider category of individuals including those working under a contract for services and partners in a partnership. In addition, other organisations, including trade unions, trade or professional associations and employment agencies, must also observe the provisions of this legislation.

Individuals who work wholly or mainly outside Great Britain are not protected by this legislation.

Please also note that when employment relationships have come to an end, the individual is still protected provided the discrimination arises out of, and is closely connected to, the employment relationship; the most obvious example would be where a former employer gives a discriminatory job reference.

Definition of sexual orientation

Sexual orientation is defined as meaning 'a sexual orientation towards persons of the same sex, persons of the opposite sex, or persons of the same sex and of the opposite sex'. This means people are protected from discrimination whatever their sexual orientation. The law does not protect individuals against discrimination relating to particular sexual practices or fetishes.

Types of discrimination

The four forms of discrimination which apply to sex and race discrimination, namely direct discrimination, indirect discrimination, victimisation and harassment, apply equally to sexual orientation discrimination.

1. Direct discrimination

Direct discrimination occurs where an employer treats an employee less favourably than it treats or would treat other people on the ground of sexual orientation. Note that it does not have to be treatment on the ground of the victim's own sexual orientation. So, for example, if a manager makes fun of a subordinate because he has a sister who is a lesbian, this could amount to direct discrimination. In addition, the definition of direct discrimination is wide enough to cover perceived, as well as actual, sexual orientation. Therefore, if an employee were to be treated less favourably because his employer thought he was gay, this could amount to discrimination even if he was not, in fact, gay.

There can be no justification in law for direct discrimination unless a genuine occupational requirement applies. This is likely to be a limited exception as it will be necessary to show that being of a particular sexual orientation is a genuine and determining occupational requirement for the job. At present it is impossible to say with any certainty the extent to which employers will be able to rely on the genuine occupational requirement exception in the context of sexual orientation, but once the law has been established for a little longer some guidance will be provided by the tribunals and courts.

2. Indirect discrimination

Broadly, the principle of indirect discrimination as examined in relation to sex and marriage discrimination applies to sexual orientation discrimination.

3. Victimisation

As with existing laws prohibiting discrimination, an employer will also be guilty of discrimination on the ground of sexual orientation by victimisation if it treats an employee less favourably than others because that employee has already or threatens to bring proceedings, give evidence or information, take any action or make any allegation concerning the employer with reference to the law prohibiting discrimination on the ground of sexual orientation.

4. Harassment

See page 97.

Exceptions to sexual orientation discrimination protection

There are three areas where exceptions to the law against sexual orientation discrimination exists:

- **National security.** Any action taken 'for the purpose of safeguarding national security' is not unlawful if it is justified for that purpose.

- **Positive discrimination.** If an employer identifies a group of persons of a particular sexual orientation as not being properly representative within certain work areas, it may try to encourage individuals of that group to apply by providing training or through an advertising campaign. This may entitle an employer to place a job advertisement in magazines targeted at gay men or women. The risk, however, is that if the employer does not have sufficient information to be able to demonstrate that individuals in that particular group are not properly represented, such an advert might constitute indirect discrimination.

- **Benefits dependent on marital status.** It is not discriminatory for an employer to provide additional benefits which are dependent upon employees being married. Take, for example, an employer introducing a private medical insurance benefit to all employees, where the benefits extend to the spouses of employees who are married. This is not discriminatory. On the other hand, if the employer provides private health insurance cover to all employees and opposite-sex partners (whether married or unmarried) but not to same-sex partners, this would be discriminatory.

Employer responsibility for discrimination

The same principle applies as previously described in relation to the SDA in the first section of this chapter. For an employer relying on this defence, regard will be given to whether a written policy of sexual orientation discrimination has been issued to employees, whether training has been given and whether disciplinary action has been taken against those guilty of sexual orientation discrimination.

Discrimination on the grounds of religion or belief

Discrimination on the grounds of religion or belief is made unlawful by the Employment Equality (Religion or Belief) Regulations 2003, which forbids such discrimination at every stage of employment (i.e. advertising vacancies, engagement of employees, promotion, training and other opportunities, and dismissal). As with other forms of discrimination, protection covers more than just employees; it protects individuals when the employment relationship has come to an end provided the discrimination arises out of, or is closely connected to, the employment relationship. Individuals who work wholly or mainly outside Great Britain are not protected by this legislation.

Definition of religion or belief

Religion or belief is defined as meaning 'any religion, religious belief or similar philosophical belief'. It is clear that people who belong to established religious traditions, such as Muslims, Jews and Catholics, will be protected by this law. However, it is not clear whether non-conventional faiths or beliefs are covered, such as humanists, atheists or Rastafarians. As the law develops, the courts and tribunals will provide guidance, but it is recommended that the following factors are considered when deciding on what is a religion or belief:

- Is there collective worship?
- Is there a clear belief system?
- Is it a profound belief affecting the way of life or the view of the world?

Please note that political opinion or belief is not included within the definition.

Types of discrimination

The four forms of discrimination, namely direct discrimination, indirect discrimination, victimisation and harassment, apply equally to discrimination on the ground of religion or belief.

1. Direct discrimination

Direct discrimination occurs where an employer treats an employee less favourably than it treats or would treat other people on the ground of that employee's religion or belief. Note that it does not have to be treatment on the grounds of the victim's own religion or belief; so, for example, if a manager makes fun of a subordinate because he associates with someone of a particular religion or belief, this could amount to direct discrimination. Also note that the complainant cannot rely on the alleged discriminator's religion or belief. In other words, if the manager was a Christian and refused to promote an employee because he was a non-believer, that employee would not have a claim for discrimination.

The definition of direct discrimination is wide enough to cover perceived, as well as actual, religion or belief. Therefore, if a man were to be treated less favourably because his employer thought he was Jewish, this could amount to discrimination even if he was not, in fact, Jewish.

There can be no justification in law for direct discrimination unless a genuine occupational requirement applies. This exception may be relevant to organisations which have an ethos based on religion or belief such as churches and denominational schools.

2. Indirect discrimination

Broadly, the principle of indirect discrimination as examined in relation to sex and marriage discrimination applies to religion or belief discrimination. What this means is that an organisation must not have any policies, rules or other practices (whether formal or informal) which have the effect of disadvantaging people of a particular religion or belief, which cannot be sufficiently justified by the need to meet a proper business requirement.

3. Victimisation

As with existing laws prohibiting discrimination, employers will also be guilty of discrimination on the grounds of religion or belief by victimisation if they treat an employee less favourably than others because that employee has already or threatens to bring proceedings, give evidence or information, take any action or make any allegation concerning the employer with reference to the law prohibiting discrimination on the grounds of religion or belief.

4. Harassment

See below.

Exceptions to religion or belief discrimination protection

There are two main areas where exceptions to the law against religion or belief discrimination exist:

- **National security.** Any action taken 'for the purpose of safeguarding national security' is not unlawful if it is justified for that purpose.

- **Positive discrimination.** If an employer identifies a group of persons of a particular religion or belief as not being properly representative within certain work areas, it may try to encourage individuals of that group to apply by providing training or through an advertising campaign. This may entitle an employer to place a job advertisement in magazines targeted at minority religions.

In addition, specific allowance is made to exempt Sikh men from the requirement to wear safety helmets while on a construction site.

Employer responsibility for discrimination

The same principle applies as previously described in relation to the SDA in the first section of this chapter. For an employer relying on this defence, regard will be given to whether a written policy of religion or belief discrimination has been issued to employees, whether training has been given and whether disciplinary action has been taken against those guilty of religion or belief discrimination.

Harassment

Racial and sexual harassment have been held to be unlawful direct discrimination by the RRA and the SDA, but until recently harassment has not been defined as a distinct offence under those Acts. The position is now changing and harassment has been defined and is unlawful on the grounds of sex, race, disability, sexual orientation and religion or religious belief.

There is an increased awareness of the issues involved in harassment, and recent years have shown a significant rise in complaints to employment tribunals. If the complaint is serious, employment tribunals will award high damages. Therefore, it is crucial for employers to take steps to prevent harassment occurring in their workplace. Where it does occur, they should deal with it appropriately.

Definition

The legal definition is that harassment occurs where, on the grounds of sex, race, disability, sexual orientation, religion or belief an employer engages in unwanted conduct which has the purpose or effect of violating an individual's dignity or creating an interrogating, hostile, degrading, humiliating or offensive environment for the individual.

This is a relatively wide definition and its scope will include physical, verbal and non-verbal conduct. The conduct must also be unwanted by the recipient, but it is irrelevant whether the harasser has a motive or intention of harassing.

Employer responsibility for harassment

Harassment falls under discrimination legislation and therefore the employer is liable for the acts of its employees in the course of their employment. It is not always clear whether an act of harassment should be regarded as 'in the course of employment'. If the harasser is acting in a supervisory role, his act of harassment is more likely to be deemed to be in the course of employment than if the harasser is in a subordinate position.

Employers, however, can avoid liability for the action of an employee in the course of employment if they can prove that they took such steps as were reasonably practicable to prevent the employee from committing a certain act or from committing acts of that description in the course of his employment. This defence has been examined earlier in this chapter.

Preventing harassment

The best way to avoid harassment complaints (whether on the grounds of sex, race, disability, sexual orientation, religion or religious belief) is to ensure that harassment does not occur in the first place. Employers should have an equal opportunities policy and a sexual and racial harassment policy which define harassment and state that it should not occur (see Appendix 14) and make reference to harassment on all the grounds listed above. Employees must be made aware of the existence of these policies, educated about harassment and warned of its consequences.

Employees should be aware that acts of harassment are taken very seriously by the employer and will be considered gross misconduct.

Dealing with harassment complaints

Complaints of harassment can be very disruptive to the workplace and must be dealt with very carefully. If an employee complains of harassment, consider whether an informal approach to the harasser would be appropriate, i.e. if it is a less serious complaint or the first instance of harassment. Consider whether the person complaining of harassment wants an informal approach or would prefer more formal action to be taken.

If an informal warning is appropriate, the alleged harasser should be consulted to explain that the conduct is upsetting the employee, that it is considered harassment and must not continue. He should also be warned that the matter will be kept under review. He must be shown the policy which is in place and warned that if matters do not improve disciplinary action will be taken. The person who has complained of harassment should be kept informed of the warning given and told to inform the employer if he has any further complaints against the alleged harasser.

Where an informal approach is inappropriate or if the complainant wants formal action to be taken, the disciplinary procedure should be followed in the following way:

- Ask the complainant for a full statement.

- Suspend the alleged harasser pending the investigation of the complaint (if appropriate).

- Take statements from all staff who can provide evidence about the alleged harassment.

- Interview the alleged harasser and invite him to provide a statement. A disciplinary hearing to give the alleged harasser the opportunity to answer the complaint or justify or excuse his conduct will be necessary if there is substance to or doubt in relation to the matters complained of.

- Very often there will be no witnesses and it will be one word against the other, leaving it to the employer to decide which version to believe.

- If the conclusion is that harassment has taken place, consider a penalty. In serious cases, the likely outcome will be dismissal although, in some circumstances, it may be appropriate to transfer the harasser. With harassment of a less serious nature, a final written warning will be appropriate.

Criminal Justice and Public Order Act 1994

Under this Act (only applicable in England & Wales), there is now a criminal offence of intentional harassment, alarm or distress which renders racial, sexual and all other forms of harassment (including harassment against homosexuals and disabled persons at work and in the street) a criminal offence punishable by six months' imprisonment or a fine of £5,000. It is necessary to prove that the harasser's action was intentional and also that someone was actually harassed.

This offence relates to harassment by an individual and is of little use in the employment context, although employers may be under a duty to inform employees of their rights under the Act.

Protection from Harassment Act 1997

Under this Act, it is now an offence for someone to pursue a course of conduct which amounts to harassment of another and which he knows, or ought to know, amounts to harassment. In addition to providing for harassers to be subject potentially to a fine or up to six months' imprisonment (can be up to five years' imprisonment for very serious cases in Scotland), the Act creates a number of civil remedies including damages and restraining orders backed by powers of arrest. In Scotland, the civil remedies include damages, interdict and non-harassment orders with powers of arrest.

Equal pay

The Equal Pay Act 1970 (EPA) provides that discrimination between the sexes in the terms of their contracts of employment is unlawful. This typically occurs in matters such as salary, bonus payments and benefits.

The EPA has been criticised because its provisions are too complex and it takes many years for claims under the Act to reach a conclusion.

The EPA protects males as well as females and it benefits employees under a contract of employment as well as self-employed people under a contract for services. It does not apply to individuals who work wholly or mainly outside Great Britain, nor does it apply to members of the armed forces.

The EOC has published a code of practice on pay which aims to provide practical guidance and includes a suggested equal pay policy.

Meaning of equality

An individual can claim equality if he can establish one of the following:

- that he is carrying out work which is the same or broadly similar to work being carried out by someone of the opposite sex in the same employment; or

- that he is carrying out work which has been rated as equal, through a job evaluation study, to work being carried out by someone of the opposite sex in the same employment; or

- that he is carrying out work which is of equal value to the work of someone of the opposite sex in the same employment.

Comparison. The comparison must be with a person of the opposite sex who exists (or has existed) who is doing similar work, work graded as equal or work of equal value and who is employed by the same employer (or an associated employer) either at the same establishment or at an establishment within Great Britain where, in general, common terms and conditions are observed.

Defence. An employer can successfully defend a claim under the EPA if it can:

- prove that the work is not like or similar, not rated as equal or not of equal value; or

- prove that the difference between the complainant's contract and the comparison contract is genuinely due to a material factor which is not the difference in sex; this requires that the employer shows the reason for the factor and that the factor identified objectively justifies the difference in the contracts.

Equality clause. If an individual can establish that one of the above three justifications for equality applies and his contract contains terms less beneficial than those enjoyed by the comparator of the opposite sex, or which omits a beneficial term enjoyed by the comparator, he can apply to an employment tribunal to have an equality clause implied into his contract. Such a clause modifies the individual's contract so that it is equivalent to the comparator's contract.

Other remedies. In addition to an equality clause in the contract, a person successful in a complaint under the EPA may be awarded compensation for loss suffered in the past as a result of lack of equality.

CHAPTER 6

Termination of employment

All employers must at some time deal with the termination of contracts of employment. Many employers associate termination of employment with the anxiety and expense of proceedings being brought against them by a disgruntled employee. This does not have to be the case if the employer is aware of the contractual and statutory duties in relation to termination so that termination can be effected in a legally acceptable way.

This chapter describes the various ways contracts of employment can be brought to an end, the potential problems that can arise and the recommended procedure for avoiding such problems. The chapter is divided into sections as follows:

- Dismissal

- Other terminations

- Claims and settlements for termination

Dismissal

In the context of termination of employment, 'dismissal' is defined as occurring in the following situations, each of which is discussed in subsequent sections:

- The employee's contract of employment is terminated by the employer with or without notice.

- The employee works under a fixed-term contract and the term expires without renewal under the same contract.

- The employee terminates his own contract, with or without notice, in circumstances such that he is entitled to by reason of the employer's conduct. This is known as 'constructive dismissal' (see page 106).

'Unfair dismissal' arises from statutory rights (see page 111 for details) whereas 'wrongful dismissal' arises from contractual rights (see page 116 for details).

Termination by employer with or without notice

Termination with notice

The proper notice to be given is often specified in the contract of employment; the written statement given to the employee must include the length of notice which the employee is obliged to give and entitled to receive (see page 17). However, if a notice period has not been expressly agreed, there is an implied term that it may be terminated upon reasonable notice. Just what is reasonable notice will depend on the case in question, taking into account the seniority, age, length of service, remuneration of the employee and what is usual in the industry.

Whatever the contractual provisions for termination of the contract, the notice actually given must not be less than the statutory minimum period of notice (see page 17). If proper notice is given, there can be no claim for wrongful dismissal. However, there may still be a valid claim for unfair dismissal if proper notice is given. Conversely, a dismissal may be fair even though proper notice is not given.

Pay in lieu of notice

It is common for an employer terminating an employment contract to want the employee to cease working immediately. This is because very often an employee who knows he is leaving will not carry out his work effectively and can be disruptive in the workplace. In these circumstances, it is usual for the employer to pay the employee a sum in lieu of notice or compensation for failure to give notice.

Sometimes the contract will provide that it may be terminated either by notice or without notice on payment of a sum in lieu. In these circumstances the employee is entitled to the pay in lieu under a contractual obligation on the employer to make the payment, and tax and National Insurance deductions should be made in the usual way.

Usually, however, there is nothing in a contract relating to making payments in lieu. In these circumstances payment may be considered as compensation for the employer's breach of contract in not giving notice and, in some circumstances, may be paid tax-free up to a limit of £30,000. But it is not always entirely clear whether payment should be seen as compensation or as payment in lieu of notice so it is worth seeking advice on this point.

When compensation is being paid free of tax, the fact that it is compensation should be stated to the employee in writing, with a condition that the employee agrees to reimburse the employer in the event that it becomes liable to pay tax in relation to the payment. See the example letter at Appendix 27 from an employer dismissing with payment in lieu of notice. If there is any doubt about whether or not the sum should be paid tax-free, clearance can be sought from the Inland Revenue in advance.

Compensation must be assessed to put the employee in the same position, with respect to damages for the employer's breach of contract of employment, as if the contract had been performed during the notice period. Therefore, it is not only the employee's salary but also all benefits, such as company car, that must be included in the calculation.

Termination without notice

Dismissal without notice is a breach of contract by the employer rendering it liable in damages for wrongful dismissal (see page 116). The exception is when the employee has acted in gross misconduct, in which case the employer is justified in dismissing with immediate effect. A contract often expresses the right of the employer to dismiss the employee without notice; but, in any event, the employer should give its employees a clear indication of what type of conduct it regards as gross misconduct. This will depend upon the type of employment in question, as conduct which constitutes gross misconduct in one area of employment might not be considered to be so serious in another. Examples may be included in the disciplinary procedure, although it should be made clear that the examples given are not exhaustive. Examples of gross misconduct are: theft, damage to the employer's property, incapacity for work due to being under the influence of alcohol or illegal drugs, physical assault and gross insubordination.

Expiry of a fixed-term contract

A fixed-term contract will automatically terminate at the end of the term, without the need for any notice to be given. However, if a fixed-term contract is not renewed, the employee may have a valid claim for redundancy pay or in respect of unfair dismissal.

A fixed-term contract can be extended where an employee remains in the employment after the expiry of the term. In these circumstances, the contract of employment will continue with an implied term that it may be terminated by either party giving reasonable notice.

Constructive dismissal

If the employer's conduct is such that it is in fundamental breach of the contract of employment, the employee may resign with immediate effect. In such circumstances the employee may have a valid claim for unfair dismissal and for wrongful dismissal.

Resigned or constructively dismissed?

Where an employee complains of unfair and constructive dismissal, it is common for the employer to argue that the employee resigned and dismissal did not occur. The employee would have to prove that the employer's conduct clearly breached and repudiated the contract entitling him to leave without notice (whether he gave notice or not).

The employee must have considered that the contract was at an end because of the employer's conduct. The employer's conduct is sufficient to justify the employee leaving and complaining of constructive dismissal if it:

- was a significant breach going to the root of the contract of employment; or

- showed that the employer no longer intended to be bound by one or more of the essential terms of the contract.

Very often constructive dismissal occurs as a result of a breach of the implied terms of trust and confidence in the contract (i.e. a breakdown in the employment relationship). This can be caused by a single action by the employer (such as verbal abuse) or by a series of less serious actions which together amount to a breach of the terms.

If an employer makes a statement of clear intention to breach an essential term of the contract, the employee can leave and claim constructive dismissal based on an anticipatory breach of the contract.

The employee must leave quickly because of the breach of contract. If he does not leave soon after the incident or incidents complained of, the employer can argue that the employee accepted the alleged breach and therefore no constructive dismissal will have occurred.

It is necessary for the employee to send a Step One letter under the statutory grievance procedure (see Appendix 10) and wait 28 days before he can bring a claim of constructive dismissal in an employment tribunal.

Other terminations

Resignation

Resignation by an employee should be with notice. The period of notice to be given by an employee is subject to a statutory minimum of one week, although the contractual notice period will in many cases be longer. The contractual notice period may be either expressly agreed upon or implied. If implied, the notice period must be considered a reasonable period under all the circumstances.

An employee is entitled to continue to receive all benefits for the notice period provided he is ready and willing to work for that period. However, the parties may agree that the employee may stop working before the end of the full notice period.

An employer is advised to ensure that clear words of resignation are used. Words spoken in the heat of the moment should not be relied upon as terminating the employment, as they may not amount to a resignation. The employment would then be deemed to be terminated by dismissal by the employer and the employee would have a right to make a claim of unfair dismissal.

The employer should accept the resignation and communicate this acceptance to the employee. Once accepted, the employee may not withdraw the resignation without the employer's consent.

It is a good idea to ask the employee why he is leaving. Answers may alert the employer to potential problems with other employees. A written note of the employee's reasons for leaving should be kept.

If an employee resigns without giving notice, he will be in breach of contract unless it is in response to a fundamental breach of contract by the employer (i.e. constructive dismissal). If the employee does resign without giving notice, the employer can contractually require the employee to serve out the period of notice which he should have given, but in practice this would be very difficult to enforce because a court may not compel an employee to work. However, the employer should not pay the employee for any time after the date of resignation. The employee is not entitled to pay in lieu of notice.

An employer may want an employee to serve out the correct period of notice to prevent the employee from immediately joining a competitor. A better way to do this may be to include a clause in the employee's contract restraining him (after leaving the employment) from working for a competitor. However, such a restriction must be for a reasonable period of time only and within a reasonable geographical distance from the former employer. Such clauses have to be carefully worded as the employee must be able to continue to earn a living. Such clauses shall only be enforceable if they are reasonably required for the protection of the employer's legitimate business interests. Alternatively, or in addition, an employer may include what is known as a 'garden leave' clause in the contract of employment. Garden leave describes the situation where an employee serving his notice of termination is required to remain at home, although he continues to be paid. The aim behind this practice is to prevent the employee from leaving to work for a competitor while not having that employee around at work where he may obtain confidential information. Employers wishing to include restrictive clauses or garden leave clauses in their contracts of employment should consult a solicitor.

Redundancy

See page 117 for details.

Mutual agreement

The parties may mutually agree to terminate the contract of employment at any time. But if it is clear that the employee was forced to agree to the termination with the threat of dismissal, he will be held to have been unfairly dismissed. Financial inducements to agree to terminate the employment are, however, fully acceptable.

If the parties mutually agree to end the contract, there is no need for the employer to give a notice of termination. There will be no entitlement to pay in lieu of notice or redundancy pay. However, it is fairly usual for the employer to make a payment described as an 'ex gratia payment' to avoid any implication of dismissal.

Retirement

If an employer requires an employee to retire at a certain age, this should be included in the contract of employment. An employee may continue in employment beyond pensionable age for as long as he is able to work, unless there is an agreed-upon retirement date or there is a recognised customary date for retirement in the trade or industry.

The right to complain of unfair dismissal and to claim a redundancy payment ceases when an employee reaches the normal retiring age of his employer or, if there is no normal retiring age, at the age of 65.

Death

Unless a contract of employment provides otherwise, the death of either party terminates the contract.

Frustration

Very rarely, 'frustration' of a contract of employment occurs if some outside event happens that is not the fault of either party to the contract. The outside event must have been unforeseen by the parties when they entered into the contract and it must make it impossible for the contract to be performed at all, or it must make its performance radically different from its original purpose. If frustration occurs, the contract is terminated automatically without any need for either party to give notice.

Examples of frustration occurring are when an employee suffers an illness and, as a result, can never work again. Frustration may also occur if the employee is sentenced to prison.

In unfair dismissal cases, employers have argued that there has been no dismissal but termination by frustration instead. It is not advisable to rely on frustration to avoid an unfair dismissal complaint, as employment tribunals do not readily accept that a contract has been terminated by frustration.

Insolvency of the employer

An employer's insolvency has the effect of terminating the contract of employment.

The employees may apply to the employer's representative for payment and if payment is not forthcoming, they may make an application to the Secretary of State for payment.

Claims and settlements for termination

In the preceding sections of this chapter, reference has been made to claims of unfair dismissal, wrongful dismissal and redundancy payments.

These are explored in further detail below to give employees an indication of their rights and employers an idea of potential liabilities and recommendations on how they might resolve these disputes.

Claims

Unfair dismissal

Dismissal of an employee without good reason, or without following a fair procedure, is likely to be unfair and liable to an unfair dismissal claim in an employment tribunal. The right not to be unfairly dismissed is a statutory right effective when the employment contract is entered into. It is subject to certain qualifying conditions.

Qualifying conditions

To bring a claim for unfair dismissal, an employee must currently have been employed under a contract for a minimum continuous period of one year from the commencement of the contract until the effective date of termination, and he must have been dismissed. In addition, he must not be over normal retirement age or, if there is no retirement age, 65.

Continuity of employment remains unbroken even if there has been a transfer of business ownership or employee absence from work because of sickness, injury, pregnancy or confinement (rules for assessing what is continuous employment are set out in sections 210 to 219 of the Employment Rights Act 1996).

The effective date of termination is either the date the notice to terminate expires, the date of the termination of employment or, if it is a fixed-term contract, the date on which it expires unrenewed. If the employer has not given the statutory minimum period of notice (except when entitled to dismiss without notice), the effective date of termination is the date when the statutory minimum period of notice to which the employee is entitled expires.

The time limit for bringing a claim for unfair dismissal is three months from the effective date of termination of the contract. An employment tribunal will extend the time limit when it is not practicable to bring the claim within this limit.

No qualifying period of service is required and there is no upper age limit if the dismissal is for:

- membership or non-membership of an independent trade union or taking part in activities of an independent trade union;

- a maternity-related reason;

- an adoption-related reason;

- a paternity-related reason;

- a health and safety reason;

- asserting statutory rights;

- the performance by an employee representative (or a candidate due to become an employee representative);

- the performance by an employee who is a pension scheme trustee;

- a shop or betting worker for refusing to work on a Sunday;

- a reason connected with the Working Time Regulations;

- a reason related to making protected disclosure (i.e. 'whistleblowing');

- a reason related to securing the benefit of the National Minimum Wage;

- enforcing a right to working family tax credits; or

- taking part in 'protected' industrial action.

An employee who is dismissed on medical grounds specified in any health and safety at work law, regulation or code of practice can make a claim for unfair dismissal provided he has one month's continuous employment.

No contracting-out

Employers cannot exclude or waive an employee's right not to be unfairly dismissed. The inclusion of such a term in a contract of employment would have no legal effect, leaving the employee at liberty to bring a complaint of unfair dismissal in the employment tribunal.

There are exceptions to this principle, and an agreement that limits the right not to be unfairly dismissed is effective:

- if the agreement is reached through a conciliation officer from ACAS (see page 119);

- if it is a valid compromise agreement (see page 120).

Reasons for dismissal

If an employee can prove that he has all the qualifying conditions to bring a claim for unfair dismissal, the employer then has to establish the reason, or principal reason (if there was more than one), for the dismissal and prove it is either:

- connected to the capability or qualifications of the employee for performing work of the kind which he was employed to do; capability is assessed by reference to skill, aptitude, health or any other physical or mental quality (Appendices 27 and 28 are examples of dismissal letters for capability and sickness – where dismissal is for one of the other reasons, these letters can be adapted accordingly);

- connected to the conduct of the employee; or

- redundancy; or

- the employee could not continue to work in the position which he held without violating (either on his part or on that of his employer) a duty or restriction imposed by or under law; or

- connected with some other substantial reason of a kind sufficient to justify the dismissal of an employee.

If the employer can satisfy the employment tribunal that the reason or principal reason for dismissal is one of the above, the tribunal will consider whether dismissal was fair or unfair. The tribunal will look at the reason given by the employer, and all the circumstances surrounding the dismissal including the size and administrative resources of the employer, in order to decide the reasonableness of the dismissal. If the employment tribunal is not satisfied that dismissal was for an acceptable reason, dismissal shall be ruled unfair.

Test of reasonableness

The decisive factor at this stage is whether or not the employer followed a fair procedure, appropriate in the circumstances, leading up to the dismissal. This is why the practice of using standard, fair procedures for the various circumstances that arise during the employment relationship can be crucial to avoid liability for unfair dismissal. Different procedures are appropriate for the different circumstances. This book includes various procedure flowcharts in the Appendices for reference (see page 174).

Automatically unfair dismissals

Dismissal is automatically unfair for:

- membership or non-membership of an independent trade union or taking part in activities of an independent trade union;

- a maternity-related reason (see pages 46–7);

- an adoption-related reason;

- a paternity-related reason;

- a health and safety reason;

- asserting statutory rights;

- the performance of an employee representative (or candidate to be an employee representative);

- the performance of an employee who is a pension scheme trustee;

- the transfer of an undertaking, i.e. where the ownership of the employer is transferred from one person/entity to another;

- a spent conviction or failure to disclose a spent conviction;

- unfair selection for redundancy, i.e. selection will be unfair if it is for any of the above reasons;

- taking parental leave or taking time off for dependants, and performing functions as an employee representative (or as a candidate to be an employee representative) for the purposes of establishing a workforce agreement in relation to parental leave;

- making a protected disclosure (i.e. whistleblowing);

- a National Minimum Wage reason;

- enforcing a right to working family tax credit; or

- taking part in protected industrial action.

Remedies

If a tribunal finds that dismissal has been unfair, it may make an order for reinstatement (for the employee to return to his original job), re-engagement (for the employee to be placed in employment comparable to that from which he was dismissed or other suitable employment) or compensation (up to a statutory maximum limit).

Compensation is the most common remedy and usually comprises a basic award and a compensatory award. Further details of these are set out below. In addition, there are further awards made in certain circumstances, such as an 'additional award' if the employer fails to comply with an order for reinstatement or re-engagement, and a 'special award' if the employer fails to comply with an order for reinstatement or re-engagement where dismissal was on the ground of trade union membership or activities, or health and safety duties.

1. Basic award

The basic award is calculated by considering the employee's age, length of continuous service and gross average weekly wage. Each completed year of service up to a maximum of 20 counts for payment on the following scale (with a maximum of currently £280 for a week's pay):

- up to 22 years of age – ½ week's pay;
- between 22 and up to 41 years of age – 1 week's pay;
- between 41 and up to 65 years of age – 1½ weeks' pay.

Where an employee is dismissed after his 64th birthday, the basic award is reduced by one-twelfth for every month after that.

The current maximum basic award is £8,400 (i.e. 1½ x 20 x 280).

A tribunal will reduce the basic award if it considers it is just and equitable to do so.

2. Compensatory award

The compensatory award is an amount the employment tribunal considers just and equitable in all the circumstances relating to the loss sustained by the employee, as a result of the dismissal. The award is calculated on the net value of wages, other benefits and expenses reasonably incurred by the employee as a result of the dismissal.

Factors an employment tribunal will take into account to reduce the award are:

- contributory fault;
- whether dismissal would have resulted even if the employer had acted reasonably;
- the employee's duty to minimise his loss by attempting to seek other employment;
- payments made by the employer;
- what is just and equitable.

Once the assessment of the compensatory award has been made, the statutory limit, which is currently £56,800 (except in cases of refusal to comply with a reinstatement or re-engagement order), must be applied. This statutory limit does not apply where the dismissal is as a result of making a protected disclosure (i.e. whistleblowing).

For dismissals that occur after 1 October 2004 the compensatory award may be increased or decreased by between 10 and 50 per cent for failure to comply with the statutory dispute resolution procedures depending upon which party is at fault (subject to the statutory cap of £56,800).

Wrongful dismissal

Wrongful dismissal is a common law remedy distinct from unfair dismissal. It occurs when an employer terminates an employee's contract of employment in a way that breaches it or the employer's conduct is such that it entitles the employee to resign (i.e. constructive dismissal). In these circumstances, the employee may take proceedings against the employer in an employment tribunal or in the civil courts (County court or the High Court in England & Wales and the Sheriff Court or Court of Session in Scotland) for wrongful dismissal, claiming damages for breach of contract.

There is no requirement for the employee to have a qualifying period of continuous employment to make such a claim.

Damages are assessed on the basis that they should put the employee in the position he would have been in had the contract been performed in accordance with its terms. They are usually assessed in accordance with the notice period by which the employer could lawfully have terminated the contract. Generally, this is subject to a duty of the employee to minimise his loss by seeking other employment. However, the employee will have no such duty if he has a contractual right (as opposed to the employer having a discretion) to pay in lieu of notice. It is recommended that advice is sought on the wording of the contract to assess whether a duty to minimise loss exists. In addition, if the employee has been dismissed in breach of a contractual disciplinary procedure, the damages may be assessed with reference to the time that it would have taken to go through the disciplinary procedure.

Employees are not entitled to damages for loss, injury to feelings or distress arising from the manner of dismissal, and generally nor are they entitled to damages for injury to reputation.

Redundancy

Employees in a redundancy situation are entitled to a statutory redundancy payment. Also, if dismissal by reason of redundancy is not effected in a reasonable way, it may amount to unfair dismissal.

Definition of a redundancy situation

A redundancy situation exists where an employee's dismissal was attributable wholly or mainly to the fact that:

- the employer has ceased, or intends to cease, to carry on the business for which the employee was employed or has ceased, or intends to cease, to carry it on at a place where the employee was employed (i.e. relocation); or

- the business's need for work for which the employee was taken on has ceased or diminished, or is expected to (i.e. a reduction in the number of employees is required).

Statutory redundancy payment

Employees in a redundancy situation are entitled to a statutory redundancy payment if they have at least two years' service after reaching the age of 18. The entitlement is calculated in the same way as the basic award for unfair dismissal claims (except employment prior to reaching 18 is not counted). The calculation is made by considering the employee's age, length of continuous service and gross average weekly wage. Each completed year of service, up to a maximum of 20 after the age of 18, counts for payment on the following scale (with a maximum of currently £280 for a week's pay):

- between 18 and up to 22 years of age – ½ week's pay;

- between 22 and up to 41 years of age – 1 week's pay;

- between 41 and up to 65 years of age – 1½ weeks' pay.

Where an employee is made redundant after his 64th birthday, the payment is reduced by one-twelfth for every month after that.

The current maximum redundancy payment is £8,400 (i.e. 1½ x 20 x 280).

An employee may raise a complaint with an employment tribunal if he has not received the correct redundancy payment. The time limit for such a claim is six months from the relevant date as defined by section 145 of the Employment Rights Act 1996 (usually the effective date of termination). The time limit may be extended for a further six months if approved by the employment tribunal.

An employee is not entitled to statutory redundancy payment if, before the existing employment ends, the employer offers him (orally or in writing) employment on the same terms or suitable alternative employment, to commence within four weeks of the ending of the original employment. If the employee unreasonably refuses such an offer, or during a trial period for the new job unreasonably terminates such employment, he loses the right to statutory redundancy payment.

If the employee leaves employment before the dismissal takes effect and the employer objects in writing, the employment tribunal may determine the extent of the employee's entitlement.

Unfair dismissal

Dismissal for redundancy may be unfair due to a failure by the employer to comply with the obligation to consult with appropriate representatives of the employees concerned. These are either representatives of an independent trade union or other elected representatives. Failure to adhere to an agreed redundancy procedure does not render a dismissal automatically unfair, but it may be relevant to the tribunal's view of the procedure actually adopted by the employer (see Appendix 26).

The amount of a basic award will be reduced by the amount of any redundancy payment awarded by a tribunal or paid by the employer in respect of the same dismissal.

An employer's failure to adhere to the standard statutory dismissal and disciplinary procedure for redundancy occurring after 1 October 2004 will render the dismissal automatically unfair and the compensatory award may be increased by 10 to 50 per cent (subject to the statutory cap of £56,800).

Settlements and arbitration

Where there is a dispute, the parties will often prefer to settle the matter rather than proceed to a hearing. A settlement agreement is only binding if either of the following courses are taken:

ACAS conciliation

One way to contract validly out of an employee's right to pursue a case to a tribunal is by means of a settlement promoted by an ACAS conciliation officer (see Appendix 20). A conciliation officer has a duty to promote a settlement once a complaint has been put to a tribunal if requested to do so by the complainant, the employee concerned, or if in the absence of such a request, the conciliation officer considers there is a reasonable prospect of achieving a settlement.

Settlements are recorded on ACAS Form COT 3, signed by the parties, containing a clause under which the complainant agrees that no further proceedings arising out of the matter will be pursued by him.

Compromise agreements

The only other way to settle a matter validly is by making a compromise agreement between the parties in full and final settlement.

For a compromise agreement to be effective, it must be in writing and must fulfil the following conditions:

- It must relate to the particular complaint.

- The employee must have received independent legal advice from a qualified lawyer, an officer of an independent trade union or a worker at an advice centre as to the terms and effect of the proposed agreement, and in particular its effects on his ability to pursue the appropriate rights before an employment tribunal. The adviser who gives the advice must have an insurance policy covering the risk of a claim by the employee for an alleged loss arising out of the advice.

- The agreement must identify the adviser.

- The agreement must declare that the above conditions are satisfied.

If none of these courses are taken, the employee shall still be at liberty to commence proceedings despite the fact that he has received a compensation payment to settle. If he does proceed to make a claim, however, the payment can be taken into account when assessing compensation.

However, if the dispute is only in relation to wrongful dismissal (i.e. it is only a contractual claim), the parties may settle validly by agreement without the need for any special requirements to be satisfied. You will find basic example compromise agreements for unfair dismissal and redundancy at Appendices 30 and 31.

ACAS Arbitration Scheme

This scheme gives parties to straightforward claims of unfair dismissal the option of having an independent arbitrator rule on the case, whose decision is final and binding and there is no right of appeal (except in very limited circumstances).

Glossary

ACAS	Advisory Conciliation and Arbitration Service. Established under the Employment Protection Act 1975 to support collective bargaining and work to improve employer/employee relations.
Action in good faith	An act carried out honestly.
Agent	A person appointed by another to act on his behalf.
Applicant	Someone who lodges a complaint with an employment tribunal.
Augment	To supplement.
Breach of contract	A failure by a party of a contract to live up to the terms agreed to in the contract or to perform the obligations delineated in the contract.
Civil wrong	A non-criminal wrong based on the denial of another person's rights.
Code of practice	Rules established by regulatory, administrative bodies, trade associations, etc, which are used to suggest and guide behaviour. These rules do not have the force of law.
Collective agreement	Agreement reached as a result of negotiations between an employer and a trade union.
Common law	Laws arising from court rulings rather than from legislative enactments.
Complainant	Someone who lodges a complaint.

Constructive dismissal	Resignation by an employee in circumstances such that he is entitled to resign by reason of an act or course of action by the employer.
Contract for service	A type of contract that defines an independent contractor.
Contract of service	A type of contract in which a person agrees to be paid a regular wage, works regular hours and considers himself to be an employee.
Contract out	Attempting to exclude or limit liability.
DDA	Disability Discrimination Act 1995. Prohibits discrimination based on disability relating to employment and access to goods, facilities, services and premises.
Discrimination	Treatment of one or more members of a specified group in a manner that is unfair as compared to the treatment of other people who are not members of that group.
EPA	Equal Pay Act 1970. Requires that men and women be paid the same rate for like employment, or work rated as equivalent or having equal value.
Ex gratia	Given as a favour. An ex gratia payment is one not required to be made by a legal duty.
Express terms	The terms and provisions of a contract that the parties specifically deal with and agree upon.
Frustration	An unexpected and unintentional event that makes the fulfilment of the terms of a contract impossible.
Gross wages	The amount of wages before any deductions are made.
Guarantee payments	The sum that an employer must pay an employee for whom he is unable to provide work, under the Employment Rights Act 1996.
Implied terms	Terms that are not expressly stated in a contract but are necessary to give it business efficacy or are derived from custom and usage.
Indemnification	One person agrees to pay to a third person money owed to him by a second person.

Legitimate interests	An employer's right to have certain interests protected by law.
Mandate	A legal order to do something.
Net wages	The amount of wages after deductions are made.
Notice	Formal advance notification by either party to an employment contract, to the other, that the contract is about to expire and will not be renewed.
PIW	Period of incapacity for work. Any period of four or more consecutive days during which the employee has been found incapable of working due to illness.
Redundancy	Termination of employment because a job no longer exists.
Remuneration	Reward or pay for service.
Repudiatory breach	A fundamental breach of contract by either the employer or the employee that entitles the other party to terminate the relationship without giving notice.
Respondent	The person against whom relief is sought by the applicant.
Restrictive covenant	A provision in a contract prohibiting certain post-employment activities on the part of an ex-employee.
RRA	Race Relations Act 1976. Prohibits discrimination based on colour, race, nationality, or ethnic or national origin in employment, services and housing.
SAP	Statutory adoption pay. An employer must pay SAP to any employee who is eligible.
SDA	Sex Discrimination Act 1975. Prohibits discrimination based on gender or marital status in employment, or when offering a contract of employment.
SMP	Statutory maternity pay. An employer must pay SMP to any employee who is eligible.
Spent conviction	A conviction that, after a specified period of time, can be treated as if it never existed and does not need to be disclosed.

SPP	Statutory paternity pay. An employer must pay SPP to any employee who is eligible.
SSP	Statutory sick pay. An employer must pay SSP to any employee who is away from work ill after the first four days of absence, up to 28 weeks.
Statement of particulars	For a written statement outlining the nature, terms, duties and responsibilities of a specific job.
Statutory rights	Any privilege recognised and protected by law.
Unfair dismissal	A remedy for unjustifiable dismissal based on statutory rights.
Winding up	A procedure by which a company liquidates its assets and dissolves itself.
Wrongful dismissal	A remedy for unjustifiable dismissal based on contractual rights.

Appendices

Appendix 1: Rehabilitation periods

Sentence	Rehabilitation periods
Imprisonment, corrective training or sentence of detention in a young offenders' institution for between six and 30 months	10 years
Imprisonment or sentence of detention in a young offenders' institution for a term not exceeding six months	7 years
A fine or sentence not expressly covered by the Rehabilitation of Offenders Act 1974	5 years
Order for detention in a detention centre	3 years
Absolute discharge	6 months
Conditional discharge (or until the order expires, whichever is longer)	1 year
Probation (or until the order expires, whichever is longer)	5 years

Note: For young offenders, periods are usually reduced by half, except in cases of probation, supervision, care-orders, conditional discharges or bind-overs, attendance centre orders and hospital orders (with or without restriction).

Appendix 2: Documents as evidence of entitlements to work in the UK

- Any document containing the National Insurance number of the person named in a document issued by the:
    - Inland Revenue
    - Benefits Agency
    - Contributions Agency
    - Jobcentre Plus
- A passport stating the holder to be a British citizen:
    - having the right to live in the UK
    - having an entitlement to re-enter the UK
- A passport issued by, or on behalf of, the UK government containing a Certificate of Entitlement to live in the UK.
- A certificate for Registration of Naturalisation as a British citizen.
- A birth certificate issued in the UK, the Republic of Ireland, the Channel Islands or the Isle of Man.
- A passport or national identity card which describes the holder as a National of the State issuing the documents, that State being a party to the European Economic Area Agreement.
- A passport or other travel document or letter from the Home Office stating that the holder is exempt from immigration control or has indefinite leave to enter or remain in the UK, or has no time limit to stay.
- A passport or other travel document or letter from the Home Office stating that the holder has current leave to enter or remain in the UK and is not precluded from taking the employment in question.
- A UK residence permit held by a European National.
- A passport or other travel document stating that the holder has a current right of residence in the UK by virtue of being a family member of a named European National in the UK.
- A letter from the Home Office stating that the named person is a British citizen or has permission to take up employment.
- A work permit or other document permitting employment issued by the Department for Education and Employment or the Training and Employment Agency.
- A passport stating that the holder is a British Dependent Territories citizen by virtue of a connection with Gibraltar.

Appendix 3: Letter inviting candidate to attend interview

Ace Fabrics Limited

Unit 2 Boxwood Trading Estate, Kings Langley, HO3 2HT
Tel: (01234) 456 789 Fax: (01234) 987 654

Dear *Miss Porter*

Thank you for sending me your application for the post of *Machinist*.

I would very much like to discuss this matter further with you and have arranged an interview at *10am* on *Wednesday 5 October 2005* at these offices. I should be grateful if you would confirm your attendance.

I look forward to meeting you.

Yours sincerely

John Smith

John Smith
Personnel Manager

Appendix 4: Rejection letter before interview

Ace Fabrics Limited

Unit 2 Boxwood Trading Estate, Kings Langley, HO3 2HT
Tel: (01234) 456 789 Fax: (01234) 987 654

Dear *Miss Porter*

I refer to your application for the post of *Machinist* with this Company.

I regret that after careful consideration you have not been selected for interview on this occasion as there were other applicants whose experience and qualifications matched our requirements more closely.

However, I would like to take this opportunity to thank you for your interest in our Company and I should like to wish you every success in your future job hunting.

Yours sincerely

John Smith

John Smith
Personnel Manager

Appendix 5: Letter of offer of employment

Ace Fabrics Limited

Unit 2 Boxwood Trading Estate, Kings Langley, HO3 2HT
Tel: (01234) 456 789 Fax: (01234) 987 654

Dear *Miss Porter*

Post of *Machinist*

Following your interview at this office on *Wednesday 5 October 2005*, I am pleased to offer you the above position with *Ace Fabrics Limited* ('the Company') subject to satisfactory references[1] and a medical report.[2] It is the Company's final decision as to whether such references meet with its requirements. You are advised not to resign from your present position until I have confirmed to you that your references have been received and are satisfactory to us. We will endeavour to obtain your references as quickly as possible.

If you accept this offer of employment, your job will be based at *Unit 2 Boxwood Trading Estate, Kings Langley, HO3 2HT.*

Your employment will commence on *Tuesday 1 November 2005* and the first four weeks will be treated as a probationary period during which time your employment may be terminated by yourself or by the Company on one week's notice.

Your duties and responsibilities will be as set out in the attached job description and you will be responsible to *Mr. Brown.*

/continued

[1] References are usually taken up at this stage, the offer being made subject to satisfactory references. See model letter of Request for Reference and notes at Appendix 6. A candidate who receives a job offer subject to satisfactory references should not resign from his current employment until all the conditions have been satisfied. In the public sector, offers are usually made unconditional only after all the conditions are met.

[2] Medical examinations of prospective employees are not a legal requirement, although employers are recommended to carry them out now that health and safety in the workplace is so important. A prospective employee is not obliged to agree to have a medical examination, although if he did refuse it would be reasonable for the prospective employer not to make an offer.

Appendix 5: Letter of offer of employment (continued)

Your basic salary at the commencement of your employment will be *£13,500 per year* payable monthly in arrears by bank credit transfer on the last day of each month. Your normal weekly hours will be from *9am to 5pm Monday to Friday with a one-hour break for lunch.*

You will be entitled to *four weeks'* holiday in every year, in addition to the normal statutory entitlement, of which no more than *two* weeks may be taken consecutively. The holiday year runs from *1 February* to *31 January*.

The Company will be entitled to terminate your appointment by giving you written notice of *one week for the first two years of service plus one week for every further year of service up to a maximum of 12 weeks.*

You are required to give the Company *one week's* notice of your intention to terminate your employment with the Company.

Your other terms of employment will be provided on your first day of employment.[3]

If you wish to accept this offer of employment, I would be grateful if you could confirm your acceptance by signing and returning one copy of this letter in the stamped addressed envelope enclosed.[4]

I do hope that you will accept this offer. In the meantime, if you wish to discuss any aspect of this offer, please do not hesitate to contact me.

Yours sincerely

John Smith

John Smith
Personnel Manager

---

[3] Alternatively, these may be set out in an enclosed statement of particulars of employment or incorporated into this letter.

[4] Once this offer has been accepted, the parties have entered into a contractual relationship and the employer will need to issue either a full contract or a statement of particulars of employment (see chapter 2).

Appendix 6: Letter of request for reference[1]

Ace Fabrics Limited

Unit 2 Boxwood Trading Estate, Kings Langley, HO3 2HT
Tel: (01234) 456 789 Fax: (01234) 987 654

Dear Sir

Re: *Miss Porter*

The above named has applied to us for the position of *Machinist* and has given us your name as a referee.[2]

We understand that *Miss Porter* was employed by you from *4 October 1993* to *21 October 2005* as a *Machinist*. We should be grateful if you would confirm that this is the case and let us know whether, in your opinion, she performed her tasks competently and conscientiously.

We should also be grateful if you would let us know whether you would consider *Miss Porter* a reliable and responsible employee. Could you also let us know the reasons why she left your employment?

We assure you that any reply you may give will be treated in the strictest confidence.[3]

/continued

---

[1] There is no legal obligation to provide a reference, although it is rare that an employer or ex-employer will refuse to supply one. If a reference is given, it should be accurate. If it is not accurate, the person who gives the reference may be liable to an action for: (a) **defamation** by the subject if the inaccuracy damages the reputation of the subject. The person who gives the reference will not be liable for defamation if he believes the information to be correct and gives it without malice; (b) **negligence** by both the subject and the recipient, both of whom could sue for damages for any financial loss arising out of a negligent reference. Wording may be included in the reference to exclude legal liability as in the model reference letter at Appendix 8.

[2] The request may be for a reference to be given over the telephone and sometimes employers or ex-employers are more willing to give fuller information than in writing. Again, there is no legal obligation to give a reference over the telephone, but if it is given, it should be accurate.

[3] All references should be marked 'private and confidential'.

Appendix 6: Letter of request for reference (continued)

A stamped addressed envelope is enclosed.[4]

Yours faithfully[5]

John Smith

John Smith
Personnel Manager

---

[4] It is customary to include a stamped addressed envelope for the return reference. The advantage of this is that the reference is returned straight to the person for whom it is intended.

[5] In addition to obtaining references, a potential employer is advised to check the prospective employee's qualifications, if possible, before the job offer is made.

Appendix 7: Rejection letter after interview[1]

Ace Fabrics Limited

Unit 2 Boxwood Trading Estate, Kings Langley, HO3 2HT
Tel: (01234) 456 789 Fax: (01234) 987 654

Dear *Miss Porter*

Thank you for attending the interview for the post of *Machinist* at this office on *Wednesday 5 October 2005*.

I regret that after careful consideration your application has been unsuccessful on this occasion as there were candidates whose qualifications and experience matched our requirements more closely.

However, I would like to take this opportunity to thank you for your interest in our Company and I should also like to wish you every success in finding a suitable post in the near future.

Yours sincerely

John Smith

John Smith
Personnel Manager

---

[1] It is a good idea to wait until the preferred candidate has accepted the offer before sending the letters of rejection to the other candidates. Subject to this, it is good practice to notify unsuccessful candidates as soon as possible.

Appendix 8: Reference letter on employee

Fabric Works Limited

Unit 17 Felsham Trading Estate
Bovingdon HP17 2LS
Tel: (01987) 789 456
Fax: (01987) 654 987

Dear *Mr. Smith*

Re: *Miss Porter*

In reply to your request for a reference for the above named, I confirm that *Miss Porter* was employed by this Company between the dates of *4 October 1993 and 21 October 2005* as a *Machinist*.

During her employment with this Company *Miss Porter* performed her tasks competently and conscientiously and I consider her to be a reliable and responsible employee. *Miss Porter* left our employment due to redundancy.

This reference is given to be of help to you and in fairness to your proposed employee. It is given on the basis that we accept no legal liability and that you must rely upon your own judgement whether or not to proceed with your proposed employment of this individual. We trust you shall hold this reference in strict confidence.

Yours sincerely

Peter Johnson

Peter Johnson
Managing Director

Appendix 9: Statement of terms and conditions of employment

Information which must be included in the principal statement:

- the names of the parties;
- the date on which employment began and the date on which any previous employment (with this or any other employer) commenced which is to be regarded as continuous with this employment;
- the scale or rate of remuneration or the method of calculating such remuneration and the frequency of payment;
- any terms and conditions relating to hours of work, including normal working hours;
- any terms and conditions relating to entitlement to holidays, including public holidays and holiday pay (sufficient to enable the employee's entitlement, including entitlement to accrued holiday pay on termination, to be precisely calculated);
- the employee's job title or a brief description of his work;
- the employee's place of work, or where the employee is required or permitted to work at various places, an indication of that fact, together with the address of the employer.

Information which must be given in writing (but which may or may not be included in the principal statement):

- where the employment is not intended to be permanent, the period for which it is expected to continue;
- where the employment is for a fixed term, the expiry date;
- the length of notice the employee is obliged to give and is entitled to receive in order to terminate his contract (or reference to the law or an accessible collective agreement);
- rules relating to sick leave and sick pay (or reference to a document where such details may be found);
- any collective agreements which directly affect the employee's terms and conditions of employment including, where the employer is not a party, the names of the parties;
- details of any pensions or pension schemes (or reference to documents where such details may be found);
- a statement of whether a contracting-out certificate is or is not in force;
- where the employee is required to work outside the United Kingdom for more than one month, the period of such service, the currency in which remuneration will be paid, and additional remuneration and/or benefits provided while working overseas and any terms and conditions of employment relating to the employee's return to the United Kingdom;
- any disciplinary rules and grievance procedures applying to the employee (or reference to documents where such details may be found). This only applies to the employer who employs over 20 employees;
- the persons to whom the employee can apply for redress of any grievances or dissatisfaction with a disciplinary decision (or reference to documents where such details may be found).

Where there are no terms to be given under any of these headings, this should be stated.

Appendix 10: Standard dispute resolution procedures

Standard Dismissal and Disciplinary Procedure

- **Step One letter:** Employer must send the employee a letter setting out the nature of the employee's conduct or capability or other circumstances which have led the employer to contemplate dismissing him or taking other disciplinary action, including the basis for the complaint.

- **Step Two meeting:** Employer must invite the employee to a meeting, which the employee must take all reasonable steps to attend. After the meeting, the employer must inform the employee about any decision and inform him of his right to appeal.

- **Step Three appeal:** If the employee wishes to appeal, the employer must invite the employee to a further meeting, which should be heard by a more senior manager where possible. After the meeting, the employer must inform the employee of the final decision.

Modified Dismissal and Disciplinary Procedure

- **Step One letter:** Employer must send the employee a letter setting out the nature of the alleged misconduct which has led to the dismissal, together with any supporting evidence, and notifying the employee of the right to appeal.

- **Step Two appeal:** If the employee wishes to appeal, the employer must invite the employee to attend an appeal meeting. After the meeting, the employer must inform the employee of the final decision.

Standard Grievance Procedure

- **Step One letter:** Employee must set out the nature of the alleged grievance in writing to the employer.

- **Step Two meeting:** Employer must invite the employee to a meeting, which the employer must take all reasonable steps to attend. After the meeting, the employer must inform the employee about its decision, and notify him of the right to appeal.

- **Step Three appeal:** If the employee wishes to appeal, the employer must invite the employee to an appeal meeting, which should be heard by a more senior manager if possible. After the meeting, the employer must inform the employee of its final decision.

Modified Grievance Procedure

- **Step One letter:** Employee must set out the nature of the alleged grievance in writing to the employer.

- **Step Two response:** Employer must set out its response in writing and send that to the employee.

Appendix 11: Employment contract

Employment Contract

THIS AGREEMENT IS MADE the *25th* day of *October 2005.*[1]

BETWEEN (1) *Ace Fabrics Limited of Unit 2 Boxwood Trading Estate, Kings Langley, HO3 2HT* (the 'Employer') and (2) *Jenny Porter of 12 Elm Drive, Milton Keynes ME9 1BA* (the 'Employee')

This document sets out the terms and conditions of employment which are required to be given to the Employee under section 1 of the Employment Rights Act 1996 and which apply at the date hereof.

1. Commencement and Job Title

The Employer agrees to employ the Employee from *1 November 2005* in the capacity of *Machinist* at *Unit 2 Boxwood Trading Estate.* No employment with a previous employer will be counted as part of the Employee's period of continuous employment.[2] The Employee's duties which this job entails are set out in the job description attached to this statement. The job description may, from time to time, be reasonably modified as necessary to meet the needs of the Employer's business.

2. Salary

The Employer shall pay the Employee a salary of £*13,500* per year payable by credit transfer at monthly intervals on the last day of each month. The Company shall review the Employee's salary at such intervals as it shall, at its sole discretion, decide.

3. Hours of Employment

The Employee's normal hours of employment shall be *9.00am* to *5.00pm* on *Mondays* to *Fridays* during which time the Employee may take up to

---

[1] This must be no later than two months after the employment commences. Any changes must be notified to the employee within one month of the change. No statement is required to be given to an employee employed under a contract for less than one month.

[2] If employment with a previous employer is to be counted as a period of continuous employment, this, and the date it began, must be stated.

one hour for lunch between the hours of *12.00pm* and *2.00pm*, and the Employee may, from time to time, be required to work such additional hours as is reasonable to meet the requirements of the Employer's business at an overtime rate of *£7.50* per hour.

4. Holidays

The Employee shall be entitled to *20* days' holiday per calendar year at full pay in addition to the normal public holidays. Holidays must be taken at times convenient to the Employer and sufficient notice of the intention to take holiday must be given to the Employee's supervisor. No more than two weeks' holiday must be taken at any one time unless permission is given by the Employee's supervisor.

The Employee shall be entitled to payment in lieu of holiday accrued due but untaken at the date of termination of his employment. If, at the date of termination, the Employee has taken holiday in excess of his accrued entitlement, a corresponding deduction will be made from his final payment.

5. Sickness

5.1 If the Employee is absent from work on account of sickness or injury, he or someone on his behalf should inform the Employer of the reason for the absence as soon as possible but no later than *12.00pm* on the working day on which absence first occurs.

5.2 *The Company reserves the right to ask the Employee at any stage of absence to produce a medical certificate and/or to undergo a medical examination.*

5.3 The Employee shall be paid normal remuneration during sickness absence for a maximum of *four weeks* in any period of *12 months* provided that the Employee provides the Employer with a medical certificate in the case of absence of more than *seven consecutive days*. Such remuneration will be less the amount of any statutory sick pay or social security sickness benefits to which the Employee may be entitled. Entitlement to

Appendix 11: Employment contract (continued)

payment is subject to notification of absence and production of medical certificates as required above.[3]

6. Collective Agreements

There are no collective agreements in force directly relating to the terms of your employment.[4]

7. Pension

The Employee shall be entitled to join the Employer's pension scheme, the details of which are set out in the Employer's booklet/leaflet which is entitled *Your Pension at Ace Fabrics* and which is available on request. A contracting-out certificate under the Pension Schemes Act is in force in respect of this employment.[5]

8. Termination

The Employer may terminate this Agreement by giving written notice to the Employee as follows:

(a)   With not less than one week's notice during the first two years of continuous employment; then

(b)   With not less than a further one week's notice for each full year of continuous employment after the first two years until the 12th year of continuous employment; and

(c)   With not less than 12 weeks' notice after 12 years of continuous employment.[6]

---

[3]   If the employer does not wish to pay normal remuneration during sickness, it should state that the statutory sick pay rules apply.

[4]   Where a collective agreement directly affects the terms and conditions of employment, the following should be inserted as clause 6: *'The terms of the collective agreement dated [ ] made between [ ] and [ ] shall be deemed to be included in this Agreement'.*

[5]   Where no pension scheme exists, this must be stated and where no contracting out certificate is in force, this must also be stated.

[6]   These are the minimum periods required by law but they may be increased by agreement.

Appendix 11: Employment contract (continued)

The Employer may terminate this Agreement without notice or payment in lieu of notice in the case of serious or persistent misconduct such as to cause a major breach of the Employer's disciplinary rules.

The Employee may terminate this Agreement by one week's written notice to the Employer.

After notice of termination has been given by either party, the Employer may in its absolute discretion give the Employee payments in lieu of all or any part of any notice; or, provided the Employee continues to be paid and to enjoy his full contractual benefits under the terms of this Agreement, the Employer may in its absolute discretion for all or part of the notice period exclude the Employee from the premises of the Employer and require that he carries out duties other than those specified in his job description or require that he carries out no duties at all until the termination of his employment.

9. Confidentiality

The Employee is aware that during his employment he may be party to confidential information concerning the Employer and the Employer's business. The Employee shall not, during the term of his employment, disclose or allow the disclosure of any confidential information (except in the proper course of his employment).

After the termination of this Agreement the Employee shall not disclose or use any of the Employer's trade secrets or any other information which is of a sufficiently high degree of confidentiality to amount to a trade secret. The Employer shall be entitled to apply for an injunction[7] to prevent such disclosure or use and to seek any other remedy including without limitation the recovery of damages in the case of such disclosure or use.

The obligation of confidentiality both during and after the termination of this Agreement shall not apply to any information which the Employee is enabled to disclose under the Public Interest Disclosure Act 1998

---

[7] An 'injunction' is called an 'interdict' in Scotland.

Appendix 11: Employment contract (continued)

provided the Employee has first fully complied with the Employer's procedures relating to such external disclosures.

10. Non-Competition

For a period of *six months*[8] after the termination of this Agreement the Employee shall not solicit or seek business from any customers or clients of the Employer who were customers or clients of the Employer at the time during the *12 months*[9] immediately preceding the termination of this Agreement.

11. Dismissal, Discipline and Grievance

The Employer's Dismissal and Disciplinary Rules and Procedure and the Grievance and Appeal Procedure in connection with these rules are set out in the Employer's *Staff Handbook* which is attached hereto.[10]

12. Notices

All communications including notices required to be given under this Agreement shall be in writing and shall be sent either by personal service or by first class post to the parties' respective addresses.

13. Severability

If any provision of this Agreement should be held to be invalid, it shall to that extent be severed and the remaining provisions shall continue to have full force and effect.

14. Staff Handbook

Further details of the arrangements affecting your employment are published in the *Staff Handbook* as issued and/or amended from time to

---

[8] The employer may choose the number of months or years that are necessary to protect its business needs, but any more than two years is likely to render this clause unenforceable at law. Also see note on terms in restraint of trade on page 34.

[9] This period should be between one and two years if it is to remain enforceable by the employer.

[10] See Appendix 14.

Appendix 11: Employment contract (continued)

time. These are largely of an administrative nature, but, so far as relevant, are to be treated as incorporated in this Agreement.

15. Prior Agreements

This Agreement cancels and is in substitution for all previous letters of engagement, agreements and arrangements (whether oral or in writing) relating to your employment,[11] all of which shall be deemed to have been terminated by mutual consent. This Agreement and the *Staff Handbook*[12] constitute the entire terms and conditions of your employment and any waiver or modification must be in writing and signed by the parties to this Agreement.

16. Governing Law

This Agreement shall be construed in accordance with the laws of *England & Wales* and shall be subject to the exclusive jurisdiction of the *English*[13] courts.

Please acknowledge receipt of this statement and your agreement to the terms set out in it by signing the attached copy of this letter and returning it to *Mr. Smith*.

IN WITNESS OF WHICH the parties hereto have signed this Agreement the day and year first above written.

SIGNED

_____   _____

Signed by or on behalf of   in the presence of (witness)
Ace Fabrics Ltd

---

[11] Where Opt-Out Agreement for Working Time Regulations purposes has already been signed, add the words *'other than an Opt-Out Agreement dated [ ]'*.

[12] Where Opt-Out Agreement referred to in footnote 13 is signed, add the words *'and the Opt-Out Agreement dated [ ]'*.

[13] Or the laws of Scotland and the Scottish courts, as appropriate.

Appendix 11: Employment contract (continued)

Name _____

Address _____

_____

Dated _____   Occupation _____

SIGNED

_____   _____
Signed by the employee   in the presence of (witness)

Name _____

Address _____

_____

Dated _____   Occupation _____

Appendix 12: Working Time Regulations 1998 Opt-Out

Working Time Regulations 1998 Opt-Out

1. Definitions

1.1 In this Agreement the following definitions apply:

'Employee'   means *Miss Porter*

'the Employer'   means *Ace Fabrics Limited* of *Unit 2 Boxwood Trading Estate, Kings Langley, HO3 2HT*

'Working Week'   means an average of 48 hours each week over a 17-week period

1.2 Unless the context requires otherwise, references to the singular include the plural and references to the masculine include the feminine and vice versa.

1.3 The headings contained in these Terms are for convenience only and do not affect their interpretation.

2. Restrictions

2.1 The Working Time Regulations 1998 provide that an Employee shall not work in excess of the Working Week unless he agrees in writing that this limit should not apply.

3. Consent

3.1 The Employee hereby agrees that the Working Week limit shall not apply to his contract of employment with the Employer.

4. Withdrawal of Consent

4.1 The Employee may end this Agreement by giving the Employer three months' notice in writing.

4.2 For the avoidance of doubt, any notice bringing this Agreement to an end shall not be construed as termination by the Employee of his contract of employment with the Employer.

Appendix 12: Working Time Regulations 1998 Opt-Out (continued)

4.3 Upon the expiry of the notice period set out in clause 4.1, the Working Week limit shall apply with immediate effect.

5. The Law

5.1 These Terms are governed by the law of England & Wales and are subject to the exclusive jurisdiction of the courts of England & Wales.[1]

Signed by the Employee

_____

Date

_____

[1] Or the laws of Scotland and the Scottish courts, as appropriate.

Appendix 13: Prescribed explanatory statement setting out statutory rights in relation to Sunday shop work

Prescribed Explanatory Statement Setting Out Statutory Rights in Relation to Sunday Shop Work

You have become employed as a shop worker and are, or can be, required under your contract of employment to do the Sunday work your contract provides for.

However, if you wish you can give a notice, as described in the next paragraph, to your employer and you will then have the right not to work in or about a shop on any Sunday on which the shop is open, once three months have passed from the date on which you give the notice.

Your notice must:

- be in writing;

- be signed and dated by you;

- say that you object to Sunday working.

For three months after you give the notice, your employer can still require you to do all the Sunday work your contract provides for. After the three-month period has ended, you have the right to complain to an employment tribunal if, because of your refusal to do Sunday work, your employer:

- dismisses you; or

- does something else detrimental to you, for example, failing to promote you.

Once you have the rights described, you can surrender them only by giving your employer a further notice, signed and dated by you, saying that you wish to work on a Sunday or that you do not object to Sunday working and then agreeing with your employer to work on Sundays or on a particular Sunday.

Appendix 14: Staff Handbook[1]

Staff Handbook

Table of contents

1. Introduction

This Staff Handbook provides you with a summary of the policies and procedures that operate in the Company. It should be read in conjunction with your contract of employment as both documents form part of your terms and conditions of employment.

---

[1] In addition to the issues covered in this Handbook, it is quite common for the Handbook to deal with a number of other matters such as the logistics of overtime, taking time off for holiday, sickness, public duties, maternity, parental leave and for taking care of dependants. These arrangements will vary according to the employer and its needs, although they will always need to be in line with statutory rules. It is recommended that advice is sought from a solicitor or from other relevant bodies who can advise on these matters before the Staff Handbook is finalised and issued to employees.

Appendix 14: Staff Handbook (continued)

To respond to the changing needs of the Company as well as changes in legislation, the policies and procedures may need to be amended from time to time and when this occurs you will be informed of these changes.

If you have any questions about this Staff Handbook, please contact your manager.

2. Equal Opportunities Policy

The Company's aim is to ensure that all of its employees and job applicants are treated equally irrespective of disability, race, colour, religion, nationality, ethnic origin, age, sex, sexual orientation or marital status. The Company shall appoint, train, develop and promote on the basis of merit and ability.

All employees have a duty, both morally and legally, not to discriminate against individuals. This means that there shall be no discrimination on account of disability, race, colour, religion, nationality, ethnic origin, age, sex, sexual orientation or marital status. Employees have personal responsibility for the practical application of the Company's Equal Opportunities Policy which extends to the treatment of members of the public and employees.

Managers and supervisors who are involved in the recruitment, selection, promotion and training of employees have special responsibility for the practical application of the Company's Equal Opportunities Policy.

The Grievance Procedure is available to any employee who believes that he may have been unfairly discriminated against.

Disciplinary action under the Disciplinary Procedure shall be taken against any employee who is found to have committed an act of unlawful discrimination. Discriminatory conduct and sexual or racial harassment shall be regarded as gross misconduct.

Appendix 14: Staff Handbook (continued)

If there is any doubt about appropriate treatment under the Company's Equal Opportunities Policy, employees should consult their manager.[2]

3. Health and Safety Policy

The Company recognises that it is responsible for ensuring, so far as is reasonably practicable, the health, safety and welfare at work of its employees. The Company believes that the pro-active management of health and safety issues is an integral part of its obligations to its employees and to the wider community. This policy statement sets out in broad terms the legal responsibilities owed by the Company and by employees in relation to health and safety issues. It will only be possible for the Company to comply with these legal obligations if both its employees and any self-employed third parties on the Company's premises understand that they are under a duty to take reasonable care for the health and safety of themselves and any of their colleagues who may be affected by their acts or omissions and that they are required to co-operate with the Company to enable the Company to perform its obligations.[3]

4. Training

The Company is committed to the continual development of all its employees. It is vital that employees possess the skills and knowledge to enable them to perform their duties effectively. Any needs should be discussed with the employee's manager on an annual basis. The Company may, in its absolute discretion, provide financial assistance for external training courses which have relevance to the employee's current or likely future duties with the Company.

---

[2] Where employers consider a more detailed policy incorporating a harassment and bullying policy to be more appropriate, they should seek guidance from the EOC, CRE or ACAS.

[3] Specific rules relating to the health and safety rules particular to the organisation need to be added here.

5. Business Expenses

Employees will be reimbursed for any fair and reasonable expenses that are incurred while conducting business on behalf of the Company. Such reimbursement will be made by the Company upon submission of an expense report approved by the employee's manager. Abuse of this right to claim expenses is considered to be gross misconduct which may result in dismissal.

6. Attendance and Timekeeping

Employees are expected to attend work punctually at the hours defined in their contract of employment. Employees must receive prior approval from their manager to leave the Company premises during working hours except during lunchbreaks. This will enable the Company to ensure that employees can be located in the event of an emergency.

7. Appearance

Employees are expected to maintain a standard of personal hygiene, appearance and dress appropriate to their job responsibilities.

8. Alcohol

The consumption of alcohol is not allowed on Company premises at any time, except where authorised by the employee's manager. No employee should report to work while under the influence of alcohol. Breach of this policy may amount to gross misconduct which may result in dismissal.

9. Smoking

Smoking on Company premises is prohibited, apart from in designated areas. Employees who do not comply with the no smoking policy will be subject to disciplinary action.

10. Use of Email and the Internet

Employees are encouraged to use email and the internet at work as a fast and reliable method of communication with significant advantages for

Appendix 14: Staff Handbook (continued)

business. However, employees need to be careful not to expose both themselves and the Company to certain risks and offences that the misuse of these facilities can cause.

<u>Use of External and Internal Email</u>

- Employees must word all emails appropriately, in the same professional manner as if they were composing a letter.

- The content of any email message sent must be neither defamatory, abusive nor illegal and must accord with the Company's Equal Opportunities Policy. Sending and receiving of obscene or pornographic or other offensive material is not only considered to be gross misconduct but may also constitute a criminal offence.

- Employees must be careful of what is said in email messages as the content could give rise to both personal liability or create liability for the Company. Employees must also avoid committing themselves, or on behalf of the Company, over the internet without having received prior and express authorisation to do so, or unless this forms part of their normal day-to-day activities and has been so authorised by the Company.

- The Company reserves the right to monitor the content of emails sent and received and may undertake monitoring of both the content and extent of use of emails. Employees wishing to send confidential, non-work-related emails should do so on their own equipment, in their own time, at their own home and should tell personal email contacts never to send any personal emails to them at work.

- Employees must ensure that they have the correct email address for the intended recipients. If employees inadvertently misdirect an email, they should contact their manager immediately on becoming

Appendix 14: Staff Handbook (continued)

aware of their mistake. Failure to do so may lead to disciplinary action being taken against them.

• Employees must not send any information that the Company considers to be confidential or sensitive over the email. The Company, in particular, considers the following information inappropriate for transmission over email: [*provide list of confidential/sensitive information*].

• The email facility is provided for business purposes only. Employees must limit personal usage to a minimum and must abide by the above guidelines concerning the content of emails. Excessive personal usage or abuse of the guidelines concerning the content of emails may lead to the withdrawal of email and internet access and/or disciplinary action which could result in dismissal.

• Employees should at all times remember that email messages may have to be disclosed as evidence at any court proceedings or investigations by regulatory bodies and therefore may be prejudicial to both their or the Company's interests. Employees should consider that hard copies of emails may be taken and backup disks may retain records of emails even when these have been deleted from the system.

• Disciplinary action under the Disciplinary Procedure shall be taken against any employee who is found to be in breach of these guidelines and depending upon the circumstances and seriousness of the breach, this may result in summary dismissal.

Use of the Internet

• Employees must not use the internet to gain unauthorised access or attempt to gain unauthorised access to computer material or private databases.

Appendix 14: Staff Handbook (continued)

- Employees must not use the internet for personal purposes whether during work hours or otherwise, as this puts an unnecessary strain upon the Company's computer network. Internet access is available purely for business use and it should be used for work-related purposes only.

- Internet access may be monitored by the Company and the Company will conduct an audit of internet usage from time to time. Should any breach of these internet guidelines be discovered, then employees may, in addition to having internet access being withdrawn, be the subject of disciplinary action which, in the case of serious breach, may result in dismissal.

- Employees may not subscribe to any news list or groups or commit themselves to receiving information from any group or body without first informing their manager. Employees are requested not to view sites which require the downloading of software from the internet, even where this would be free of charge, without the prior approval of their manager. Staff are reminded of the risk of computer viruses.

- Employees must not attempt to download or retrieve illegal, pornographic, liable, sexist, racist, offensive or unlawful material. Attempts to access such material will constitute a disciplinary offence and, in addition to access to the internet being withdrawn, the member of staff may be subject to disciplinary action which may result in dismissal.

- Information on the internet may not have been placed there with the owner's permission. Therefore, employees must obtain the permission of the copyright owner before transmitting, copying or downloading such information. Where the copyright owner's consent has clearly been given, employees must comply with any terms and conditions stipulated concerning the downloading of such information.

- Information may contain viruses and therefore should not be downloaded from the internet without first obtaining the approval of *Mr. Smith* and/or instructions from *Mr. Smith* concerning the downloading of such information which must be followed. Employees should only download such information which is required for a business purpose. The downloading of information of whatever nature for personal purposes is not permitted.

11. Use of Telephones and Other Facilities

The Company's telephones, mail, faxes and photocopying facilities are provided for business purposes only. Employees must limit personal usage to a minimum. Excessive personal usage may lead to the withdrawal of email and internet access and/or disciplinary action which could result in dismissal.

12. Acceptance of Gifts

Employees must not accept directly or indirectly any payment or any other benefit or thing of value of more than nominal value from any supplier or customer or from anyone else with any actual or prospective business relationship with the Company.

Friendships may develop between customers and employees. However, any relationship between a customer and an employee which is likely to jeopardise business relations in the Company is not acceptable.

Employees must use their common sense to avoid any actual relationships.

13. Data Protection Policy

Employees may be required to give certain information relating to themselves in order that the Company may properly carry out its duties,

Appendix 14: Staff Handbook (continued)

rights and obligations as the employer. The Company will process and control such data principally for personnel, administrative and payroll purposes.

The term 'processing' may include the Company obtaining, recording or holding the information or data or carrying out any set of operation or operations on the information or data, including organising, altering, retrieving, consulting, using, disclosing or destroying the information or data. The Company will adopt appropriate technical and organisational measures to prevent the unauthorised or unlawful processing or disclosure of data.

[It may be necessary to transfer data relating to employees outside of the UK in order that the Company may properly carry out its duties, rights and obligations, in the following circumstances and to the following countries: *France, USA, etc.*]

Employees are requested to sign the attached consent form giving consent to the Company to process data relating to them which may include sensitive data.[4]

14. Whistleblowing Policy

Employees may, in properly carrying out their duties, have access to, or come into contact with, information of a confidential nature. Their terms and conditions provide that except in the proper performance of their duties, employees are forbidden from disclosing or making use of, in any form whatsoever, such confidential information. However, the law allows employees to make a 'protected disclosure' of certain information. In order to be 'protected', a disclosure must relate to a specific subject matter (listed below) and the disclosure must also be made in an appropriate way.

---

[4] Because of the far-reaching implications of the Data Protection Act 1998, employers need to develop a data protection policy that is incorporated into the Staff Handbook. This policy needs to address the issues that arise from the data protection legislation and also how they relate to the particular employer's business.

If, in the course of employment, an employee becomes aware of information which he reasonably believes tends to show one or more of the following, he must use the Company's Disclosure Procedure set out below:

- that a criminal offence has been committed, is being committed or is likely to be committed;

- that a person has failed, is failing or is likely to fail to comply with any legal obligation to which he is subject;

- that a miscarriage of justice has occurred, is occurring or is likely to occur;

- that the health or safety of any individual has been, is being or is likely to be endangered;

- that the environment has been, is being or is likely to be damaged;

- that information tending to show any of the above is being, or is likely to be, deliberately concealed.

Disclosure Procedure

Information which an employee reasonably believes tends to show one or more of the above should promptly be disclosed to his manager so that any appropriate action can be taken. If it is inappropriate to make such a disclosure to the manager, the employee should speak to *Mr. Jones.*

Employees will suffer no detriment of any sort for making such a disclosure in accordance with this Procedure. However, failure to follow this Procedure may result in disclosed information losing its 'protected status'. For further guidance in relation to this matter or concerning the use of the Disclosure Procedure generally, employees should speak in confidence to *Mr. Jones.*

15. Dismissal and Disciplinary Rules and Procedure

1. The Company's aim is to encourage improvement in individual performance and conduct. Employees are required to treat members of the public and other employees equally in accordance with the Equal Opportunities Policy. This Procedure sets out the action which will be taken when disciplinary rules are breached.

2. Principles:

(a) The list of rules is not to be regarded as an exhaustive list.

(b) The Procedure is designed to establish the facts quickly and to deal consistently with disciplinary issues. No disciplinary action will be taken until the matter has been fully investigated.

(c) At every stage employees will have the opportunity to state their case and have a right to be accompanied by a fellow employee or a trade union official of their choice at the hearings.

(d) When the Company is contemplating dismissal for disciplinary or non-disciplinary grounds, statutory dispute resolution procedures will be adopted. Where the Company is contemplating taking disciplinary action (other than a warning) statutory dispute resolution procedures will also be adopted.

(e) Only a director has the right to suspend or dismiss. An employee may, however, be given a verbal or written warning by his immediate superior.

(f) An employee has the right to appeal against any disciplinary decision.

3. The Rules:

    Breaches of the Company's disciplinary rules which can lead to disciplinary action are:

    -   failure to observe a reasonable order or instruction;

    -   failure to observe a health and safety requirement;

    -   inadequate timekeeping;

    -   absence from work without proper cause (including taking parental leave dishonestly);

    -   theft or removal of the Company's property;

    -   loss, damage to or misuse of the Company's property through negligence or carelessness;

    -   conduct detrimental to the interests of the Company;

    -   incapacity for work due to being under the influence of alcohol or illegal drugs;

    -   physical assault or gross insubordination;

    -   committing an act outside work or being convicted for a criminal offence which is liable adversely to affect the performance of the contract of employment and/or the relationship between the employee and the Company;

    -   failure to comply with the Company's Equal Opportunities Policy.

4. The Procedure:

    (a) <u>Oral warning</u>

        If conduct or performance is unsatisfactory, the employee will be given a formal oral warning, which will be recorded. The

Appendix 14: Staff Handbook (continued)

warning will be disregarded after six months' satisfactory service.

(b) Written warning

If the offence is serious, if there is no improvement in standards, or if a further offence occurs, a written warning will be given which will include the reason for the warning and a note that, if there is no improvement after 12 months, a final written warning will be given.

(c) Final written warning

If conduct or performance is still unsatisfactory, or if a further serious offence occurs within the 12-month period, a final written warning will be given making it clear that any recurrence of the offence or other serious misconduct within a period of 12 months will result in dismissal.

(d) Dismissal

If there is no satisfactory improvement or if further serious misconduct occurs, the employee will be dismissed.

(e) Gross misconduct

If, after investigation, it is confirmed that an employee has committed an offence of the following nature (the list is not exhaustive), the normal consequence will be dismissal without pay or pay in lieu of notice:

- Theft of or damage to the Company's property.

- Incapacity for work due to being under the influence of alcohol or illegal drugs.

- Physical assault and gross insubordination.

- Discrimination or harassment contrary to the Company's Equal Opportunities Policy.

While the alleged gross misconduct is being investigated, the employee may be suspended, during which time he will be paid the normal hourly rate. Any decision to dismiss will be taken by the employer only after a full investigation.

(f) Appeals

An employee who wishes to appeal against any disciplinary decision must do so to *Mr. Jones* within two working days. The employer will hear the appeal and decide the case as impartially as possible.

16. Grievance Procedure

1. The following Procedure shall be applied to settle all disputes or grievances concerning an employee or employees of the Company (but excluding those relating to redundancy selection).

2. Principles:

(a) It is the intention of both parties that employees should be encouraged to have direct contact with management to resolve their problems.

(b) The Procedure for resolution of grievances and avoidance of disputes is available if the parties are unable to agree a solution to a problem.

(c) Should a matter be referred to this Procedure for resolution, both parties should accept that it should be progressed as speedily as possible, with a joint commitment that every effort will be made to ensure that such a reference takes no longer than seven working days to complete.

Appendix 14: Staff Handbook (continued)

(d) Pending resolution of the grievance, the same conditions prior to its notification shall continue to apply, except in those circumstances where such a continuation would have damaging effects upon the Company's business.

(e) It is agreed between the parties that where the grievance is of a collective nature, i.e. affecting more than one employee, it shall be referred initially to (b) of the Procedure.

(f) If the employee's immediate supervisor/manager is the subject of the grievance and for this reason the employee does not wish the grievance to be heard by him, it shall be referred initially to (b) of the Procedure.

3. The Procedure:

(a) Where an employee has a grievance, he shall raise the matter with his immediate supervisor/manager. If the grievance concerns the performance of a duty by the Company in relation to an employee, the employee shall have a right to be accompanied by a fellow worker or trade union official if he makes a request to be so accompanied.

(b) If the matter has not been resolved at (a), it shall be referred to a more senior manager or director and the shop steward, full-time trade union officer or fellow employee, if requested, shall be present. A statement summarising the main details of the grievance and the reasons for the failure to agree must be prepared and signed by both parties.

(c) In the event of a failure to agree, the parties will consider whether conciliation or arbitration is appropriate. The Company may refer the dispute to the Advisory Conciliation and Arbitration Service, whose findings may, by mutual prior agreement, be binding on both parties.

Appendix 14: Staff Handbook (continued)

I, *Jenny Porter*, confirm that I have read and understand this Staff Handbook and accept that it forms part of my terms and conditions of employment.

_____   _____

Signed   **Dated**

Appendix I

DATA PROTECTION CONSENT FORM

I hereby consent to information relating to me being processed by the Company in order that it may properly carry out its duties, rights and obligations as my employer. I understand that such processing will principally be for personnel, administrative and payroll purposes.

I understand that information about me shall include information of a sensitive personal nature including information concerning:

[*my racial or ethnic origin*]

[*my political opinions*]

[*my religious beliefs or other beliefs of a similar nature*]

[*my membership or non-membership of a trade union*]

[*my physical or mental health or condition*]

[*my sex life*]

[*any commission or alleged commission by me of any offence*], or [*any proceedings for any offence committed or alleged to have been committed by me, the disposal of such proceedings or the sentence of any court in such proceedings*].[5]

---

[5] An employer should only include those categories that are relevant to it.

Appendix 14: Staff Handbook (continued)

I also understand that the term 'processing' includes the obtaining, recording or holding of information or data or carrying out any operation or set of operations on the information or data, including organising, altering, retrieving, consulting, using, disclosing, combining or destroying the information or data.

I confirm that I have read and understood this explanation of the processing of data relating to me by the Company and that I consent to the processing of such data.

[*I consent to the Company transferring the data outside of the UK for the following purposes:*

[*list reasons*].]

_____   _____
Signed   Dated

Appendix 15: Notification to employees being laid off and regarding guarantee payments[1]

Ace Fabrics Limited

Unit 2 Boxwood Trading Estate, Kings Langley, HO3 2HT
Tel: (01234) 456 789 Fax: (01234) 987 654

Dear *Miss Porter*

I refer to our meeting on *12 January 2005*.

As I explained at that meeting, we regret that because of economic pressure we have no option but to lay you off from work.

The period of lay-off shall take effect from *19 October 2005* and shall continue until *20 November 2005*. You shall receive guarantee payments of £18.40 per day for the first five days of this period.[1]

I very much regret that we have been forced to take this action, but I should like to assure you that we are working hard to ensure that the period of lay-off is kept to a minimum.

Yours sincerely

John Smith

John Smith
Personnel Manager

---

1   See pages 17–18 for an explanation of the rules relating to employees being laid off and guarantee payments.

Appendix 16: Public duties that employees are permitted time off to perform

- As a justice of the peace.

- As a member of a local authority.

- As a member of the Broads Authority.[1]

- As a member of any statutory tribunal.

- As a member of a board of visitors or a visiting committee.

- As a member of a National Health Service trust, a Regional Health Authority, an Area Health Authority, a District Health Authority, a Family Practitioner Committee or a Health Board.

- As a member of the managing or governing body of an educational establishment maintained by a local education authority or a school council or the governing body of a designated institution or a central institution.

- As a member of the governing body of a grant-maintained school.

- As a member of the governing body of a further education corporation or higher education corporation.

- As a member of a school board or of the board of management of a self-governing school.

- As a member of the board of management of a college of further education.

- As a member of the National Rivers Authority or a river purification board.

[1] An authority with responsibilities for conservation and recreation on the Norfolk Broads.

Appendix 17: Alterations to terms of employment

Ace Fabrics Limited

Unit 2 Boxwood Trading Estate, Kings Langley, HO3 2HT
Tel: (01234) 456 789 Fax: (01234) 987 654

To: *Miss Porter*   Date: *4 October 2005*[1]
         12 Elm Drive
         Milton Keynes ME9 1BA

This letter is to let you know that the terms and conditions of your contract have been amended as set out below.

If you wish to discuss any of these changes or require any further information, please let me know.

Date changes effective: *1 October 2005*
New wages/salary: *£13,500 per annum*
New hours of work: *8.30am* to *5.00pm*
New location: *Wessex Trading Estate, High Wycombe*
Changes to duties and responsibilities: *None*

Please acknowledge receipt of this letter and your agreement to the terms set out in it by signing the attached copy of this letter and returning it to *Mr. Smith*. You should retain the top copy with your contract of employment.

Signed:

_____

for Ace Fabrics Limited

I, *Miss Porter*, acknowledge that I have received a statement of alteration to the particulars of my employment as required by section 1 of the Employment Rights Act 1996 and agree to the terms set out in that statement.

Signed _____   Dated _____

---

[1] This must be no later than one month after the change to the terms of employment.

Appendix 18: Letter acknowledging notification of maternity leave

Ace Fabrics Limited

Unit 2 Boxwood Trading Estate, Kings Langley, HO3 2HT
Tel: (01234) 456 789 Fax: (01234) 987 654

Dear *Jenny*

Thank you for informing me of your pregnancy and the date that your baby is due. I am writing to you about your maternity leave and pay.

You are eligible for *26 weeks' ordinary maternity leave.*[1]

You have told me that you would like to begin your maternity leave on *6 October 2005.* If you want to change this date, you must notify me 28 days before the new intended start date or, if that is not reasonably practicable, as soon as you can. Your maternity leave period will end on *5 April 2006.*

If you want to come back to work before this date, you **must notify me 28 days before your new intended return date or, if that is not reasonably practicable, as soon as you can**. This is a legal requirement, but obviously it helps with planning. If you don't give notice, the Company has the right to postpone your return for 28 days from the date you informed me that you would like to return early.

If you decide that you do not want to return to work, you will be required to give four weeks' written notice in accordance with your contract of employment.

You are *eligible for 26 weeks' statutory maternity pay.*[2]

/continued

---

[1] Or, if the employee is entitled to additional maternity leave, replace with *'52 weeks' maternity leave (26 weeks' ordinary maternity leave plus 26 weeks' additional maternity leave)'*.

[2] If the employee is not eligible, state *'not eligible for statutory maternity pay'*.

Appendix 18: Letter acknowledging notification of maternity leave (continued)

The Company will pay you for six weeks at 90 per cent of your average weekly earnings, calculated based on a legal formula, which I have calculated as *£350 per week*. The Company will then pay you the standard rate of statutory maternity pay of *£106* for the remaining 20 weeks.[3]

During your period of maternity leave, you may wish to keep in touch to discuss and plan for your return. That would be helpful. I am happy to discuss the above and any other aspects of your maternity entitlements.

Yours sincerely

John Smith

John Smith
Personnel Manager

[3] If the employee is not entitled to statutory maternity pay, replace with '*I have given you Form SMP1, which explains why you do not qualify for statutory maternity pay. You may, however, be entitled to maternity allowance. If you take this form to a Benefits Agency, it will discuss your entitlements with you*'.

Appendix 19: Letter acknowledging notification of adoption leave

---

Ace Fabrics Limited

Unit 2 Boxwood Trading Estate, Kings Langley, HO3 2HT
Tel: (01234) 456 789 Fax: (01234) 987 654

Dear *Jenny*

Thank you for informing me of your intention to adopt a child and the date that your child is due to be placed with you. I am writing to you about your adoption leave and pay.

You are eligible for 52 weeks' adoption leave (26 weeks' ordinary adoption leave plus 26 weeks' additional adoption leave).

You have told me that you would like to begin your adoption leave on *6 October 2005*. If you want to change this date, you must notify me 28 days before the new intended start date or, if that is not reasonably practicable, as soon as you can. Your adoption leave period will end on *5 October 2006*.

If you want to come back to work before this date, you must notify me 28 days before your new intended return date or, if that is not reasonably practicable, as soon as you can. This is a legal requirement, but obviously it helps with planning. If you don't give this notice, the Company has the right to postpone your return for 28 days from the date you informed me that you would like to return early.

If you decide that you do not want to return to work, you will be required to give four weeks' written notice in accordance with your contract of employment.

You are *eligible for 26 weeks' statutory adoption pay*.[1]

/continued

---

[1] If the employee is not eligible, replace with '*not eligible for statutory adoption pay*'.

Appendix 19: Letter acknowledging notification of adoption leave (continued)

The Company will pay you the standard rate of statutory adoption pay of £106.[2]

During your period of adoption leave you may wish to keep in touch to discuss and plan for your return. That would be helpful. I am happy to discuss the above and any other aspects of your adoption entitlements.

Yours sincerely

John Smith

John Smith
Personnel Manager

---

[2] If the employee's average weekly earnings are less than £106, replace figure with '*90 per cent of your average weekly earnings which has been calculated as [insert figure]*'. If the employee is not entitled to statutory adoption pay, replace with '*I have given you Form [•] which explains why you do not qualify for statutory adoption pay. You may, however, be able to seek financial support from [•]. If you take this form to [•], they will discuss your entitlements with you*'.

Appendix 20: Tribunals, courts and official bodies

1. Employment tribunals

Employment tribunals determine applications relating to employment rights, the most important of which are the rights not to be unfairly dismissed; the right to a redundancy payment; the right not to be unlawfully discriminated against on the grounds of sex, race or disability in relation to employment; and rights in relation to breaches of contract. The procedure is less formal than that of a court. Cases heard in tribunals may result in awards of compensation, reinstatement or re-engagement.

2. Employment Appeal Tribunal (EAT)

The EAT is a division of the High Court, presided over by a High Court judge. It hears appeals from the decisions of the employment tribunals on questions of law. Appeals from the EAT are to the Court of Appeal (or the Court of Session in Scotland) and from there to the House of Lords.

3. European Court of Justice

Where the decision of a case depends upon a question of European law and the answer to the question is not clear, the tribunal or court can refer the matter to the European Court of Justice.

4. Advisory Conciliation and Arbitration Service (ACAS)

ACAS was established, and its activities are regulated, by UK legislation. The principal function of ACAS is to promote the improvement of industrial relations, in particular by exercising its functions in relation to the settlement of trade disputes. It provides advice to employers, employers' associations, workers or trade unions on any matters concerned with the wide range of industrial relations services, including conciliation, arbitration, mediation, and general and specific advice on industrial relations matters. ACAS may charge fees to those who benefit from the exercise of its functions. Fees are charged at present only for certain publications and seminars, and thus not for the key function of conciliation. ACAS also produces codes of practice and guidance on matters of industrial relations practice. Employment tribunals may take account of the provisions of such codes of practice when determining the fairness of a dismissal.

For addresses, see Appendix 32.

Appendix 21: Capability procedure (for responding to an employee's poor performance)

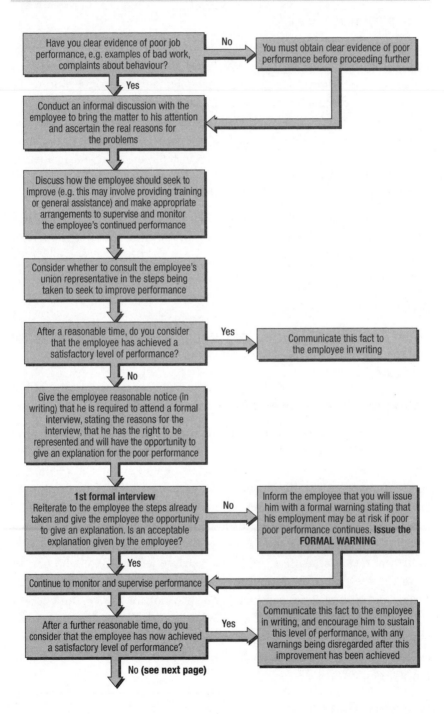

Have you clear evidence of poor job performance, e.g. examples of bad work, complaints about behaviour?

No → You must obtain clear evidence of poor performance before proceeding further

Yes ↓

Conduct an informal discussion with the employee to bring the matter to his attention and ascertain the real reasons for the problems

Discuss how the employee should seek to improve (e.g. this may involve providing training or general assistance) and make appropriate arrangements to supervise and monitor the employee's continued performance

Consider whether to consult the employee's union representative in the steps being taken to seek to improve performance

After a reasonable time, do you consider that the employee has achieved a satisfactory level of performance?

Yes → Communicate this fact to the employee in writing

No ↓

Give the employee reasonable notice (in writing) that he is required to attend a formal interview, stating the reasons for the interview, that he has the right to be represented and will have the opportunity to give an explanation for the poor performance

1st formal interview
Reiterate to the employee the steps already taken and give the employee the opportunity to give an explanation. Is an acceptable explanation given by the employee?

No → Inform the employee that you will issue him with a formal warning stating that his employment may be at risk if poor poor performance continues. **Issue the FORMAL WARNING**

Yes ↓

Continue to monitor and supervise performance

After a further reasonable time, do you consider that the employee has now achieved a satisfactory level of performance?

Yes → Communicate this fact to the employee in writing, and encourage him to sustain this level of performance, with any warnings being disregarded after this improvement has been achieved

No (see next page) ↓

Appendix 21: Capability procedure (for responding to an employee's poor performance) (continued)

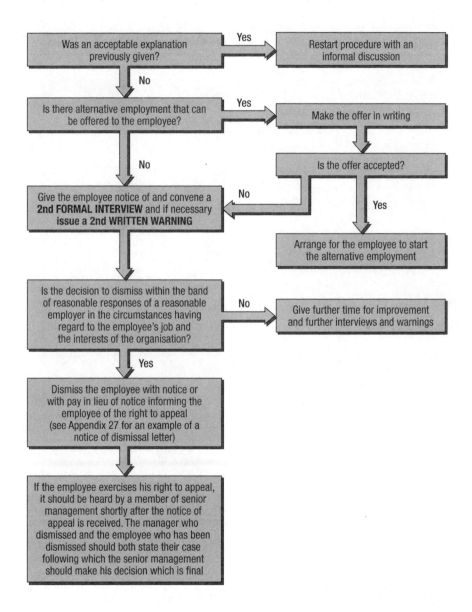

Appendix 22: Sickness procedure (for responding to an employee's prolonged absence or frequent short absences)

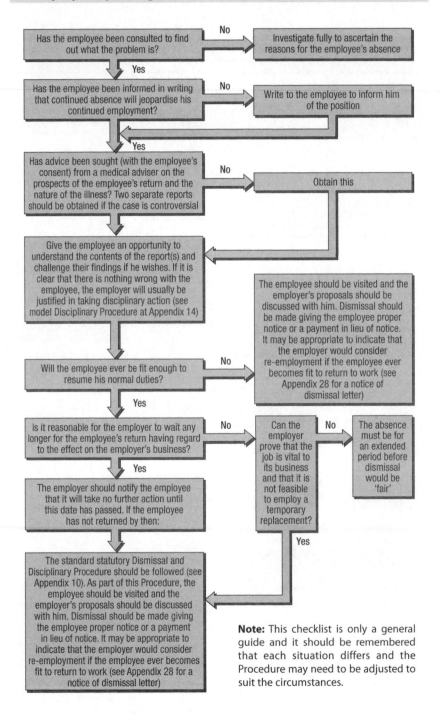

Note: This checklist is only a general guide and it should be remembered that each situation differs and the Procedure may need to be adjusted to suit the circumstances.

Appendix 23: Procedure for dealing with lack of qualifications

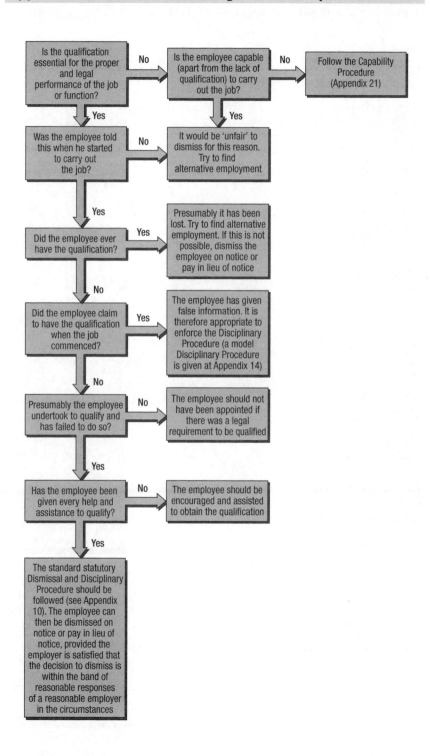

Appendix 24: Misconduct procedures (for breach of the employer's disciplinary rules)

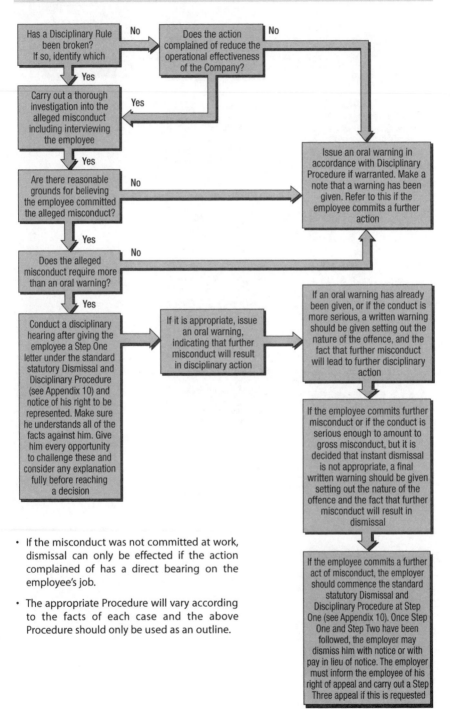

- If the misconduct was not committed at work, dismissal can only be effected if the action complained of has a direct bearing on the employee's job.

- The appropriate Procedure will vary according to the facts of each case and the above Procedure should only be used as an outline.

Appendix 25: Gross misconduct procedures (for responding to conduct warranting instant dismissal)

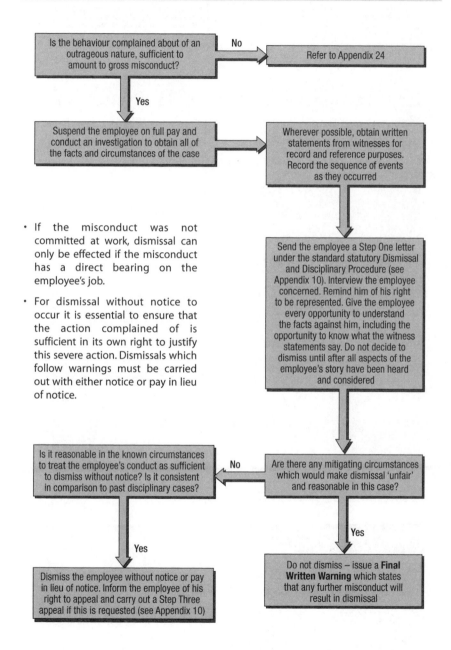

Is the behaviour complained about of an outrageous nature, sufficient to amount to gross misconduct?

No → Refer to Appendix 24

Yes ↓

Suspend the employee on full pay and conduct an investigation to obtain all of the facts and circumstances of the case

→ Wherever possible, obtain written statements from witnesses for record and reference purposes. Record the sequence of events as they occurred

- If the misconduct was not committed at work, dismissal can only be effected if the misconduct has a direct bearing on the employee's job.

- For dismissal without notice to occur it is essential to ensure that the action complained of is sufficient in its own right to justify this severe action. Dismissals which follow warnings must be carried out with either notice or pay in lieu of notice.

Send the employee a Step One letter under the standard statutory Dismissal and Disciplinary Procedure (see Appendix 10). Interview the employee concerned. Remind him of his right to be represented. Give the employee every opportunity to understand the facts against him, including the opportunity to know what the witness statements say. Do not decide to dismiss until after all aspects of the employee's story have been heard and considered

Is it reasonable in the known circumstances to treat the employee's conduct as sufficient to dismiss without notice? Is it consistent in comparison to past disciplinary cases?

← No — Are there any mitigating circumstances which would make dismissal 'unfair' and reasonable in this case?

Yes ↓ (left)   Yes ↓ (right)

Dismiss the employee without notice or pay in lieu of notice. Inform the employee of his right to appeal and carry out a Step Three appeal if this is requested (see Appendix 10)

Do not dismiss – issue a **Final Written Warning** which states that any further misconduct will result in dismissal

Appendix 26: Redundancy procedures

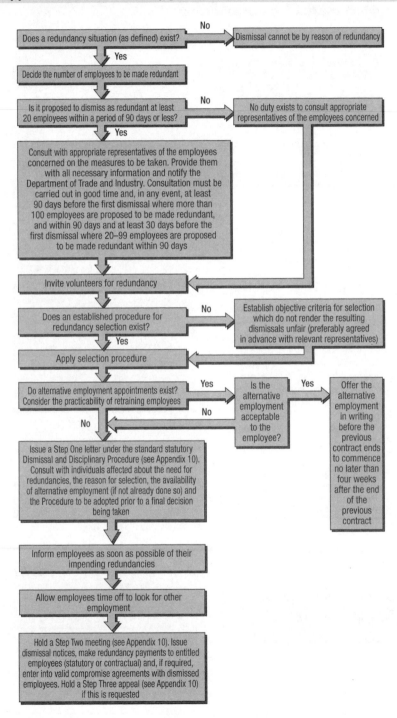

Appendix 27: Notice of dismissal letter (capability)

Ace Fabrics Limited

Unit 2 Boxwood Trading Estate, Kings Langley, HO3 2HT
Tel: (01234) 456 789 Fax: (01234) 987 654

Dear *Miss Porter*

I refer to our meeting on *11 October 2005*.

As I explained at the meeting, you have been unable to carry out your duties to the standards required by the Company. Therefore, we have no alternative but to terminate your employment with the Company with effect from *11 November 2005*.

As you are aware, we have provided you with training and assistance to enable you to improve your performance but without success. In addition, we have attempted to find suitable alternative employment within the Company but regret that nothing is available.

You are entitled to be paid in full, including any accrued holiday pay, during your notice period.

I take this opportunity of reminding you that you are entitled to appeal against this decision through the Company's Disciplinary Procedure. If you wish to exercise this right, you must let me know within two working days of receipt of this letter.

It is with regret that we have had to take this action. We should like to thank you for your past efforts for the Company and wish you every success for the future.

Yours sincerely

John Smith

John Smith
Personnel Manager

Appendix 28: Notice of dismissal letter (sickness)[1]

Ace Fabrics Limited

Unit 2 Boxwood Trading Estate, Kings Langley, HO3 2HT
Tel: (01234) 456 789 Fax: (01234) 987 654

Dear *Miss Porter*

I refer to our meeting at your home on *14 October 2005*.

I was very sorry to hear that your condition has not improved and that it is unlikely that you will be able to resume working.

As we discussed, there is little we can do to assist your return to work and our medical adviser has reported that you are not likely to be well enough to return to your current job for some time, if at all. We have tried to find some alternative suitable work for you, but, as you know, all of the work in this Company is fairly heavy work and there is nothing we can offer you.

I regret that I have no alternative other than to give you notice to terminate your employment with the Company with effect from *18 November 2005*.

You are entitled to full pay for the period of your notice plus accrued holiday pay. I shall arrange for these sums to be paid to you, and for your P45 to be sent to you as soon as possible.

If your health does improve in the future to enable you to resume working, I would be pleased to discuss re-employing you.

Yours sincerely

John Smith

John Smith
Personnel Manager

---

[1] This letter is an example of dismissal due to terminal illness. Such a letter would have to be reworded if the employee was likely to be able to resume work at some future date.

Appendix 29: Notice of redundancy letter

Ace Fabrics Limited

Unit 2 Boxwood Trading Estate, Kings Langley, HO3 2HT
Tel: (01234) 456 789 Fax: (01234) 987 654

Dear *Miss Porter*

It is with regret that I write to inform you that the Company has decided to make you redundant with effect from today. You are aware that the Company is being restructured and the volume of work has substantially diminished.

We have tried to find you a suitable position commensurate with your abilities elsewhere within the Company, but there is nothing available.

You are entitled to *one month's* notice of termination, but we believe it is better for you and all others concerned if you leave immediately. The Company will pay you a gross sum of £*1,223.39* as compensation for the termination of your employment subject to such deductions as the Company is required to make from the sum in respect of any tax charges or levies. This sum is calculated as follows:

1. *4 weeks' gross salary at £13,500 per annum*   £1,038.46

2. *5 days' accrued holiday*   £184.93

In addition, the Company will make you a statutory redundancy payment of £1,260. This is calculated in accordance with your age, salary (subject to a statutory maximum of £280 per week) and the number of years' service with the Company, i.e.:

1½ x £280 x 3

1. The Company will therefore pay you a total sum of £*2,483.39*

/continued

Appendix 29: Notice of redundancy letter (continued)

immediately on your signature and return of the enclosed copy of this letter.

2. You accept that this payment made by the Company is in full and a final settlement of your claim for compensation and/or damages for the termination of your employment with effect from today.[1]

3. You will return all property in your possession belonging to the Company.

Please acknowledge receipt of this letter by signing and returning the acknowledgement on the enclosed copy of this letter.

Yours sincerely

John Smith

John Smith
Personnel Manager

I acknowledge receipt of the letter of which the above is a copy and of the compensation payment referred to in it.

Signed _____

Date of Signature _____

---

[1] A compromise agreement is needed to prevent the employee from bringing proceedings in an employment tribunal.

Appendix 30: Compromise agreement (unfair dismissal)

Ace Fabrics Limited

Unit 2 Boxwood Trading Estate, Kings Langley, HO3 2HT
Tel: (01234) 456 789 Fax: (01234) 987 654

Dear *Miss Porter*

I hereby confirm the terms we have agreed in relation to the termination of your employment with *Ace Fabrics Limited* ('the Company') with effect from *21 October 2005*.

1. The Company will pay you without admission of any liability whatsoever the sum of *£2,000* payable immediately on your return of the enclosed copy of this letter as compensation in respect of the claims referred to in paragraph 2 of this letter.

2. You assert that you may have claims (and therefore could bring proceedings) against the Company for any of the following claims. However, you agree to refrain from initiating any proceedings *before an employment tribunal alleging that the Company dismissed you unfairly, discriminated against you on the grounds of race, sex, sexual orientation, religion or belief, or disability or has made an unlawful deduction from your wages*, and to withdraw any such proceedings now in progress.[1]

3. You accept that this payment made by the Company is in full and a final settlement of all of the claims referred to in paragraph 2 of this letter and all claims of any kind which you may be entitled to make against the Company, its officers, shareholders or employees immediately on your signature and return of the enclosed copy of this letter.

/continued

---

[1] It is necessary to relate to the particular proceedings or claims that the individual may have and this paragraph will therefore need to be amended on a case-by-case basis.

Appendix 30: Compromise agreement (unfair dismissal) (continued)

4. You will return all property in your possession belonging to the Company on or before *21 October 2005*.

5. You agree to pay any tax due in respect of the sums referred to above or to reimburse the Company for any tax the Company is required to pay in respect of such sums.

6. You agree to keep the terms of this Agreement confidential.

7. We hereby state that the conditions regulating this Agreement under *section 203 of the Employment Rights Act 1996*, under *section 77 of the Sex Discrimination Act 1975*, under *section 72 of the Race Relations Act 1976*, under *regulation 35 and schedule 4 of the Employment Equality (Sexual Orientation) Regulations 2003*, under *regulation 35 and schedule 4 of the Employment Equality (Religion or Belief) Regulations 2003* and under *section 9 of the Disability Discrimination Act 1995*[2] are satisfied. You, in turn, acknowledge and understand that you are required to take independent legal advice from a qualified lawyer on the terms and effect of this Agreement. The qualified lawyer who provides you with independent legal advice is required to sign the acknowledgement on the enclosed copy of this letter.

Please signify your acceptance of the above by signing and returning the acknowledgement on the enclosed copy of this letter.

Yours sincerely

John Smith

John Smith
Personnel Manager

---

[2] Delete irrelevant Acts as appropriate.

Appendix 30: Compromise agreement (unfair dismissal) acknowledgement

Acknowledgement

I acknowledge receipt of the letter of which the above is a copy and of the sum of *£2,000* referred to in it.

I confirm that I have taken independent advice from *John Black of Black & Brown Solicitors* of *2 High Street, Maidenhead, Berkshire* and I confirm and agree to the terms set out in the letter.

Signed _____

Date of Signature _____

I, *John Black of Black & Brown Solicitors*, confirm that *Miss Porter* has received independent legal advice within the meaning of section 203(4) of the Employment Rights Act 1996 as to the terms and effect of these terms of the letter of which the above is a copy and in particular its effect on her ability to pursue her rights before an employment tribunal.

I also confirm that I have advised *Miss Porter* in respect of all claims and prospective proceedings that she has or may have against the Company (as defined in paragraph 2 of this letter) arising out of or in connection with her employment or its termination **EITHER** [I am, and was at the time I gave the advice referred to, a Solicitor of the Supreme Court,[1] holding a current Practising Certificate and there is, and was at the time I gave the advice, in force a policy of insurance covering the risk of a claim by *Miss Porter* in respect of any loss arising in consequence of the advice I gave] **OR** [I confirm that I am competent to give this advice and am authorised to do so by (*insert trade union/advice centre*).

/continued

---

[1] Alternatively, a solicitor holding a current Practising Certificate in Scotland.

Appendix 30: Compromise agreement (unfair dismissal) acknowledgement (continued)

I further confirm that there is in force a policy of insurance which covers the risk of a claim by *Miss Porter* in respect of any loss arising in consequence of the advice I give.].[2]

Signed _____

---

[2] The Employment Rights (Dispute Resolution) Act 1998 sets out the people qualified to give relevant independent advice for the purposes of concluding valid compromise agreements. In addition to qualified lawyers, officers (or officials, employees or members) of an independent trade union and workers at advice centres (such as Citizens Advice Bureaux) can now sign compromise agreements. However, they must still be covered by a policy of insurance or an indemnity against negligent advice provided by a professional body. The letter should be amended according to who is providing the advice.

Appendix 31: Compromise agreement (redundancy)

Ace Fabrics Limited

Unit 2 Boxwood Trading Estate, Kings Langley, HO3 2HT
Tel: (01234) 456 789 Fax: (01234) 987 654

Dear *Miss Porter*

It is with regret that I write to inform you that the Company has decided to make you redundant with effect from *21 October 2005*. You are aware of, and we have discussed, the reasons for your redundancy.

We have tried to find you a suitable position commensurate with your abilities elsewhere within the Company, but there is nothing available.

The Company has, however, decided to make you an ex gratia payment of £2,000 as compensation for the termination of your employment. In addition, the Company will make you a statutory redundancy payment of *£1,260*.

The statutory redundancy payment is calculated in accordance with your age, salary (subject to a statutory maximum of £280 per week) and the number of years' service with the Company, i.e.:

1½ x £280 x 3

1. The Company will therefore pay you without admission of any liability whatsoever a total sum of *£3,260* payable immediately on your return of the enclosed copy of this letter as compensation in respect of the claims referred to in paragraph 2 of this letter.

2. You assert that you may have claims (and therefore could bring proceedings) against the Company for any of the following claims. However, you agree to refrain from initiating any proceedings *before an employment tribunal alleging that the Company has dismissed you*

/continued

Appendix 31: Compromise agreement (redundancy) (continued)

unfairly, discriminated against you on the grounds of race, sex, sexual orientation, religion or belief, or disability or has made an unlawful deduction from your wages, and to withdraw any such proceedings now in progress.[2]

3. You accept that this payment made by the Company is in full and a final settlement of all of the claims referred to in paragraph 2 of this letter and all claims of any kind which you may be entitled to make against the Company, its officers, shareholders or employees in connection with your employment or its termination including any claims which are now proceeding before an employment tribunal.

4. You will return all property in your possession belonging to the Company on or before *21 October 2005.*

5. You agree to pay any tax due in respect of the sums referred to above or to reimburse the Company for any tax the Company is required to pay in respect of such sums.

6. You agree to keep the terms of this Agreement confidential.

7. We hereby state that the conditions regulating this Agreement under *section 203 of the Employment Rights Act 1996,* under *section 77 of the Sex Discrimination Act 1975,* under *section 72 of the Race Relations Act 1976,* under *regulation 35 and schedule 4 of the Employment Equality (Sexual Orientation) Regulations 2003,* under *regulation 35 and schedule 4 of the Employment Equality (Religion or*

/continued

---

2 It is necessary to relate to the particular proceedings or claims that the individual may have and this paragraph will therefore need to be amended on a case-by-case basis.

Appendix 31: Compromise agreement (redundancy) (continued)

Belief) Regulations 2003 and under *section 9 of the Disability Discrimination Act 1995*[3] are satisfied. You, in turn, acknowledge and understand that you are required to take independent legal advice from a qualified lawyer on the terms and effect of this Agreement. The qualified lawyer who provides you with independent legal advice is required to sign the acknowledgement on the enclosed copy of this letter.

Please signify your acceptance of the above by signing and returning the acknowledgement on the enclosed copy of this letter.

Yours sincerely

John Smith

John Smith
Personnel Manager

[3] Delete irrelevant Acts as appropriate.

Appendix 31: Compromise agreement (redundancy) acknowledgement

Acknowledgement

I acknowledge receipt of the letter of which the above is a copy and of the sum of £3,260 referred to in it.

I confirm that I have taken independent advice from *John Black of Black & Brown Solicitors* of *2 High Street, Maidenhead, Berkshire* and I confirm and agree to the terms set out in the letter.

Signed _____

Date of Signature _____

I, *John Black of Black & Brown Solicitors*, confirm that *Miss Porter* has received independent legal advice within the meaning of section 203(4) of the Employment Rights Act 1996 as to the terms and effect of these terms of the letter of which the above is a copy and in particular its effect on her ability to pursue her rights before an employment tribunal.

I also confirm that I have advised *Miss Porter* in respect of all claims and prospective proceedings that she has or may have against the Company (as defined in paragraph 2 of this letter) arising out of or in connection with her employment or its termination **EITHER** [I am, and was at the time I gave the advice referred to, a Solicitor of the Supreme Court,[1] holding a current Practising Certificate and there is, and was at the time I gave the advice, in force a policy of insurance covering the risk of a claim by *Miss Porter* in respect of any loss arising in consequence of the advice I gave] **OR** [I confirm that I am competent to give this advice and am authorised to do so by (*insert trade union/advice centre*).

/continued

[1] Alternatively, a solicitor holding a current Practising Certificate in Scotland.

**Appendix 31: Compromise agreement
(redundancy) acknowledgement (continued)**

I further confirm that there is in force a policy of insurance which covers the risk of a claim by *Miss Porter* in respect of any loss arising in consequence of the advice I give.].[2]

Signed _____

---

[2] The Employment Rights (Dispute Resolution) Act 1998 sets out the people qualified to give relevant independent advice for the purposes of concluding valid compromise agreements. In addition to qualified lawyers, officers (or officials, employees or members) of an independent trade union and workers at advice centres (such as Citizens Advice Bureaux) can now sign compromise agreements. However, they must still be covered by a policy of insurance or an indemnity against negligent advice provided by a professional body. The letter should be amended according to who is providing the advice.

Appendix 32: Useful addresses

Advisory Conciliation and Arbitration Service (ACAS)
Head Office
Brandon House
180 Borough High Street
London SE1 1LW
Helpline: 0845 747 4747
Website: www.acas.org.uk

Advisory Conciliation and Arbitration Service (ACAS) – Scottish Division
151 West George Street
Glasgow G2 7JJ
Tel: 0141 248 1400

Commission for Racial Equality (CRE)
Head Office
St Dunstan's House
201–211 Borough High Street
London SE1 1GZ
Tel: 020 7939 0000
Website: www.cre.gov.uk

Department of Trade and Industry
DTI Enquiry Unit
1 Victoria Street
London SW1H 0ET
Tel: 020 7215 5000
Email: dti.enquiries@dti.gsi.gov.uk
Website: www.dti.gov.uk

Disability Rights Commission
FREEPOST MID02164
Stratford upon Avon CV37 9BR
Tel: 0845 762 2633

Textphone: 0845 762 2644
Website: www.drc-gb.org

Employment Appeal Tribunal
Audit House
58 Victoria Embankment
London EC4Y 0DS
Tel: 020 7273 1040
Website: www.employmentappeals.gov.uk

Employment Appeal Tribunal – Scottish Division
52 Melville Street
Edinburgh EH3 7HS
Tel: 0131 225 3963

Employment Tribunal Central Enquiries
100 Southgate Street
Bury St Edmunds IP33 2AQ
Tel: 0845 795 9775
Website: www.employmenttribunals.gov.uk

Equal Opportunities Commission
Arndale House
Arndale Centre
Manchester M4 3EQ
Tel: 0845 601 5901
Website: www.eoc.org.uk

European Commission
8 Storey's Gate
London SW1P 3AT
Tel: 020 7973 1992
Website: www.cec.org.uk

Appendix 32: Useful addresses (continued)

European Court of Justice

Cour de justice des Communautés
européennes
L-2925 Luxembourg
Tel: 00 352 430 31
Website: www.curia.eu.int

Health and Safety
Executive Books

PO Box 1999, Sudbury
Suffolk CO10 2WA
Tel: 01787 881 165
Website: www.hsebooks.co.uk

Health and Safety
Executive's Infoline

Caerphilly Business Park
Caerphilly CF83 3GG
Helpline: 0870 154 5500
Email: hseinformationservices@
natbrit.com
Website: www.hse.gov.uk

Home Office

Work Permits (UK)
PO Box 3468
Sheffield
Tel: 0114 259 4074
Email: wpcustomers@ind.home
office.gsi.gov.uk
Website: www.workingintheuk.
gov.uk

Jobcentre Plus Secretariat

Correspondence Manager
Ground Floor, Steel City House
West Street
Sheffield S1 2GQ

Tel: 0845 601 2001 (*employers*)
    0845 606 0234 (*job seekers*)
Website: www.jobcentreplus.gov.uk

Office of the Information
Commissioner

Data Protection Commissioner
Wycliffe House
Water Lane
Wilmslow SK9 5AF
Tel: 01625 545 700
Website: www.information
commissioner.gov.uk

Race Relations Employment
Advisory Service

4th Floor, 2 Duchess Place
Hagley Road
Birmingham B16 8NS
Tel: 0121 452 5447/8/9

Index